Grits AND Grace

COOKBOOK

A CELEBRATION OF STRONG SOUTHERN WOMEN

JUNIOR SERVICE LEAGUE
LaGRANGE, GEORGIA

GRITS AND GRACE

By Junior Service League of LaGrange

Additional copies of GRITS AND GRACE may be obtained through the
Junior Service League of LaGrange, GA website: www.jsloflagrange.com

Junior Service League of LaGrange
P.O. Box 2195 • LaGrange, Georgia 30240
www.jsloflagrange.com

About the Artist

Signe Grushovenko is a nationally recognized painter who has made her home in LaGrange for more than a dozen years. Her abstracted, figurative images are inspired by vintage photographs. After studying art at LaGrange College, Signe opened Gallery 155 in Pine Mountain, Georgia, which closed its doors in 1998. That same year, she became one of the founding members of LaGrange's Artists in Residence gallery. Married to ceramic artist Genna Grushovenko, she and her husband can be found most days at Artists in Residence, where they are both resident artists. She is also proud to show her works with successful galleries in Atlanta, Knoxville and Asheville. In recent years, she has been honored with numerous awards at shows and festivals throughout Georgia and has been featured at the Period Gallery in Omaha, Nebraska, the LaGrange National Biennial, and the "Art with a Southern Drawl" exhibition at the University of Mobile in Alabama. Her exhibitions include a one-woman show entitled "Common Roots" in Kiev, Ukraine, and a two-person show with her husband at the Annex at the Touchstone Gallery in Washington, DC. Her work, resume and contact information are available online at www.galleryair.com/signe.htm.

Artists in Residence, 300 S. Greenwood Street, LaGrange GA 30240
706-885-9900

WIMMER
COOKBOOKS

A CONSOLIDATED GRAPHICS COMPANY

800.548.2537 wimmerco.com

INTRODUCTION

"Who would have known how much work goes into creating a cookbook?" A dozen or so women are scattered around the kitchen table of the cookbook committee chairperson. The smart ones who arrived early claimed the real seats with everyone else perched on countertops, bar stools and a short stepladder.

"But isn't that the case with just about everything in life," the unlucky committee member on the ladder asks? "If someone had told me how hard raising children would be, I might have opted for chinchillas. At least they wouldn't talk back to me."

"Amen," another woman choruses. "Why didn't someone enlighten me when I decided to open my own business? I never thought I'd be up until two in the morning doing bookkeeping."

"And what was I thinking when I had the bright idea to go back to school," asks another committee member? The chairman nods knowingly and murmurs her own "Mmm, hmm" as she begins to pass out the agenda for the evening's meeting. Commiserating completed, the women get down to the business of creating a cookbook with exceptional taste.

As much as sharing recipes for the foods we love, the goal of Grits and Grace is to celebrate the spirit of strong Southern women. Throughout our history, women have taken on the tasks before them despite insurmountable obstacles, restrictive stereotypes and overwhelming odds. And even when we know the road ahead is long and hard, we march on.

Just as our favorite ingredients come together to create delicious meals, the spice and substance of gritty and graceful women are a melding of elements into something outstanding. A cup of determination, a tablespoon of courage, a dash or two of humor added in the right order at just the right time produce the unforgettable events in the lives of extraordinary women.

Enjoy our favorite recipes, but also join us around the table as we share the stories of the women of LaGrange, Georgia, as they reveal their recipes for living life with grit and grace.

COOKBOOK COMMITTEE

Cookbook Chair
Kerri Vice 2002-2005

Jessica Morman 2006-2007

Cookbook Co-Chair
Sarah Pelham 2002-2005

Stephanie Welch Downs

2006-2007

Design Chair
Casey Kornek

Taste Testing Chair
Carla Collins

Marketing Chair
Laura Erickson

Research Chairs
Heather Franklin

Diane Harrell

Typing Chairs
Martha Allred

Jessica Morman

Proofing Chairs
Stephanie Welch Downs

Shelley Strickland

Contributing Writers
Catherine Holmes

Shelley Strickland

Sustainer Advisor
Marty Young

GUEST CHEFS

Karen Scarborough

Established in 1994, Thyme Away Bed & Breakfast is located just a few blocks off the main square in LaGrange. "Come Home to Thyme Away" is more than just a slogan, it is our business philosophy. Offering a genteel alternative to lodging for business and personal travel, we want our guests to feel at home, whether they are here for a week or a night. The circa 1840 house has been lovingly restored and updated to provide guests with the experience of a past era, while providing modern conveniences comparable with more traditional accommodations.

Tulla White

LaGrange has been Tulla's hometown all of his life. His parents and grandmother owned restaurants in LaGrange, Mildred's and Sam White's. Tulla and his wife, Christy now own 3 restaurants of their own: The Basil Leaf, Venucci, and Tulla's Bayou Bar and Grill along with our catering service Tulla White Cuisine and Catering. They are the proud parents of 3 boys age 9, 7, & 4.

Anise Morrison

Anise Morrison, Chef and owner of First Catering, Inc. in LaGrange, Georgia. First Catering, Inc. owns Ou la' la' cafe in downtown LaGrange.

Anise is an artist by trade. She lived and studied at Parson's School of Design in NYC and in the south of France. Anise graduated from LaGrange College with a Bachelor of Art and Design and Art Education degrees in 1992.

Having worked in her own design business and as Creative Director on Multimedia Studios at Milliken Design Center in LaGrange, Georgia, Anise left corporate America to pursue the food business full time in 2003. Having already launched her father's recipe for the best Yam Good™ Sweet Potato Pie in Fall of 2002 and opening ou lá lá, a sweets, chocolate and coffee shop, Anise was well on her way in pursuit of fulfilling her family dreams.

Anise inherited First Catering, Inc when her father passed away in January 2001.The company was founded by Anise's parents, Jane and George E. Morrison, Jr. in 1979 when the family owned and operated several restaurants and catering business in Atlanta, Ga. She grew up in Greenville, Georgia and was reared surrounded by the food business and true "southern" great cooks. To honor the passing of recipes from grandmother to mother to daughter, Anise introduced the "Georgia Lady"® line of fine desserts, such as the family favorite of pecan pie and coconut custard. The story of the "Pie Lady" and the story of Anise's family was featured on the Food Network's, "Recipe for Success," an Al Roker production.

Anise's natural artistic abilities and travel experiences in Europe and throughout the US have influenced the design, flavors and direction of the products and menus she creates. Anise's culinary teachings are life long, worldwide and the natural desire to bake, create and share fine foods.

John W. Bell

John Bell, Pastry Chef of First Catering, Inc. and ou la' la' cafe in downtown LaGrange, Georgia. John studied at Florida State University, gained an Early Childhood Education degree from Thomas University in Thomasville, Georgia. He pursued his Master's at the University of West Georgia in Carrollton, GA.

John grew up in the small southern town of Meigs, Ga. Surrounded by a large family, food was always important and there his love of food began.

John found his way to mid- Ga for studies in teaching school but realized that his passion lay in the science of food creation. Pursuing instruction in fine pastries, chocolates, desserts, John has studied under the fine Pastry Chef Nicholas Lodge and Chef Keegan Gerhard. He travels continuously in pursuit of education on the finest techniques and newest inspirations in the field of pastry.

John joined First Catering, Inc. and ou la' la full time in the fall of 2005. Since joining the company and ou la' la', the culinary showcase of fine desserts continues to amaze and delight all who are tempted to indulge.

Jamie Keating, CEC

Jamie Keating is a graduate of Paul Smiths College in the Adirondacks of New York and The Culinary Institute of America Greystone Campus. Jamie is a member of the US National Culinary Olympic Team and a recent Gold Medalist in The World Cup, Luxembourg 2006 as well as The Salon Culinare Mondial 2005. He is the owner and chef for Gourmet Events the premier catering company that manages The RiverMill Event Centre in Columbus, Georgia. Jamie's past adventures in the culinary world have included working for Milliken and Company, Hyatt Hotels of Atlanta, Hilton Head and New Brunswick, New Jersey. His travels have taken him to Germany, Luxembourg, Switzerland and France where he worked in a Michelin 3 star Restaurant, Arpege and while in France he studied at the Le Cordon Bleu cooking school. Jamie is married to the beautiful Melissa and is the proud father of the boisterous Christopher, Nicholas and Jack, and the adorable Katie.

Kerri Vice

Kerri Vice is the owner and chef of Table Toppers Catering Co. After spending years of enjoying her passion for baking and entertaining for friends and family, she decided to start her business. Table Toppers specializes in making small parties, intimate gatherings, and celebrations special and seamless. Kerri didn't plan on using her mechanical engineering degree from Auburn University to build cakes, but it helps! She enjoys the challenge of creating cakes that will wow a crowd, while maintaining the most important aspect of great taste.

Kerri lives in LaGrange, Georgia with her wonderful husband, Coleman and their beautiful daughter, Campbell.

Robert Standard

Robert Standard started his culinary career at the Milliken Guest House in Spartanburg, SC and moved to LaGrange in 1989 to be the Executive Chef at the Guest House here. In 1997, he opened Life of the Party Catering and in 2000 Events on Main, a special events facility. In business with Robert is Mike Patterson. He moved to LaGrange from Belton, SC in 1989 to pursue a career in sales. With the opening of Events on Main, he left sales to become the events facility's manager. Together Robert and Mike have opened Kazan. Open in 2007, Kazan is the product of a rapidly changing market in the newly revitalized LaGrange, GA downtown area. It is a restaurant and video bar featuring tapas, unique sandwiches and salads. The primary entertainment is music video in different genres and will showcase live musical groups and dinner theatre. The restaurant can also be rented for private parties.

Betty Daniel

Betty Daniel bought an old house, dating back to about 1860, moved it to a vacant lot on Morgan Street in LaGrange. It was here she opened her restaurant, Taste of Lemon. She had moved several homes as well as a church, and though some were lost to a fire in 2005, she has continued to keep the doors of her restaurant open. To this day customers flock from all around to sample the traditional Southern food with a distinctive flavor that is only served at Taste of Lemon.

Special Thanks goes to country historian, Clark Johnson, and the entire staff of the Troup County Archives who helped to bring to light the many strong women featured in Grits and Grace.

TABLE OF CONTENTS

About LaGrange and the League

"America's Greatest Little City," LaGrange, Georgia, is located just 70 miles south of Atlanta. The town has earned its nickname by way of a charming downtown, vibrant industrial and historic districts, an active arts community, impressive medical and educational facilities, and a strong tradition of philanthropy. All delivered with an air of Southern grace and hospitality.

Since 1973, LaGrange's civic and cultural landscape has been enriched by the Junior Service League of LaGrange. From the early days when 12 charter members and 30 founding members launched the community's first initiative for learning disabled children, the League has grown to more than 200 members strong. League members have started or supported dozens of community projects, and League dollars have made a difference in organizations as diverse as the Humane Society, the Recycling Center, the Chattahoochee Valley Art Museum, the Boys and Girls Club, the Senior Center and more.

Through fundraisers such as this cookbook, which is a sequel to our original *Southern Born and Bread* cookbook, League members have contributed well over $500,000 to their community, matching financial support with the priceless gift of volunteer service.

Today, the League actively supports programs in the arts, schools and neighborhoods of LaGrange. Funds from the sale of this cookbook, combined with the League's continuing commitment to volunteerism, will pave the way for a new century of service and enable the Junior Service League of LaGrange to continue making a difference in "America's Greatest Little City."

Appetizers

COURAGE

CIVIL WAR WOMEN FIGHT FIRE WITH FIRE

During the Civil War, a courageous group of LaGrange women displayed extreme grace under fire. It's thanks to these rifle-toting ladies that most of the town's antebellum homes were left standing after the war. Determined to protect their families and homes from the ravages of the Northern army, a group of LaGrange women organized a militia company in 1861. They called themselves the "Nancy Harts," in honor of Georgia's Revolutionary War heroine who single-handedly defended her home against invading British soldiers. (After preparing a dinner British soldiers ordered her to cook, Nancy Hart seized one of their rifles, shot one soldier who made a move for his gun and held the rest at bay until help arrived.)

When the Nancy Harts first met for their twice weekly target practice, they didn't exactly live up to the marksmanship of their namesake. Many had a bad habit of closing their eyes just before shooting, naturally causing them to miss their targets entirely. After months of practice, their marksmanship improved, but not before one wild shot killed a bull in a neighboring pasture. Along with their militia duties, the women tended to wounded soldiers arriving regularly by train after 1863, as well as cared for their families while their husbands were off at war.

In the end, all their hard work paid off. In 1865, when Federal soldiers marched into LaGrange, they were met by the Nancy Harts. Captain Nancy Morgan informed the Federal colonel the women were determined to defend their families and homes. In response, the colonel promised to do no harm to LaGrange's homes or peaceful citizens if the women would disarm. The Nancy Harts agreed. Even under the pressures of war, the Nancy Harts never forgot their Southern hospitality. That evening, to thank the colonel for his mercy, they invited him to dinner. The women of LaGrange cooked all night to literally make enough food for an army.

Appetizers

Artichoke Dip

1	round loaf white bread	1	(16 ounce) carton sour cream
2	tablespoons butter	1	(12 ounce) package shredded
	Small bunch green onions		Cheddar cheese
4	cloves garlic, finely minced	1	can artichoke hearts, drained
1	(8 ounce) package cream		and cut into small pieces
	cheese, room temperature		

Cut the top off and hollow out center of bread. Melt butter over low hear and sauté onions and garlic until onions wilt. Combine with all other ingredients. Add all to the bread bowl. Wrap twice in heavy duty aluminum foil and bake at 350 degrees for 2 hours.

Bacon Artichoke Bundles

1	(12-16 ounce) package bacon	1	(14 ounce) can artichoke
2	cups honey mustard		hearts (not marinated)
			Toothpicks

Slice strips of bacon in half. Spread one side of bacon with mustard. Drain artichoke hearts and place a piece artichoke at one end of bacon. (If hearts are too large, slice into quarters.) Roll and secure with a toothpick. Place 1 inch apart on pan. Bake at 375 degrees for 30 to 45 minutes turning once after 20 minutes. Place on paper towel to drain. Serve hot.

Hot Feta Artichoke Dip

1	can artichokes	½	cup Parmesan cheese
2	cartons feta cheese	1	jar diced pimentos
1	cup mayonnaise	1	clove garlic, minced

Mix all ingredients together. Spread in pie dish or other similar sized dish. Bake at 350 degrees for 25 to 30 minutes.

Southern Caviar

4	cans black-eyed peas	1	bunch scallions, chopped
1	(16 ounce) can shoe peg corn	3	tomatoes, chopped
1	cup chopped bell pepper	1	cup chopped jalapeños
1	cup chopped onion	1	cup Italian dressing

Drain first 2 ingredients. Combine all ingredients and refrigerate overnight.

Southerners serve this with Frito scoops.

Brie with Amaretto and Walnuts

1	(10 ounce) round of Brie	½	cup coarsely copped walnuts
½	cup packed brown sugar		Assorted crackers, bread and
¼	cup Amaretto liqueur		apple slices

Preheat oven to 450 degrees. Remove the top rind of the Brie. Place in a shallow baking dish. Mix brown sugar, Amaretto and walnuts. Spread over top of cheese. Bake 8 to 10 minutes or until cheese melts. Keep warm and serve with assorted crackers, breads and apples.

Most serving bowls are the wrong size for mixing dips. Stir the dip in a mixing bowl and transfer it to a serving dish.

Southwestern Black Bean Dip

2 (14¾ ounce) cans black beans, drained	1 avocado, chopped
1 (14¾ ounce) can corn, drained	1 small to medium purple onion, chopped
1 (4 ounce) can black olives, chopped	1½ teaspoons salt (or to taste)
3 minced garlic cloves	½ teaspoon pepper (or to taste)
2-3 Roma tomatoes, chopped and seeds discarded	1 tablespoon sugar
	¼ cup red wine vinegar (or to taste)
	1 lime, juiced

Combine all ingredients and mix well. Better if made 12 hours prior to eating.

This is an excellent accompaniment to Cilantro Chicken (see Entrées)

Cream Cheese Crab Ball

1 (8 ounce) package cream cheese	½ cup ketchup
1 (7½ ounce) can king crabmeat	2 tablespoons horseradish sauce
Garlic powder or garlic salt	1 tablespoon lemon juice
	Assorted crackers

Drain and shred crabmeat. Mix thoroughly with cream cheese adding a few shakes of garlic powder. Form mixture into a ball. Mix together ketchup, horseradish and lemon juice. Pour over crab ball just before serving. Serve with crackers.

Christmas Cheese Ball

CHEESE BALL

1	(8 ounce) package cream cheese, room temperature	1	clove minced garlic
1	tablespoon grated onion	½	teaspoon dill

TOPPING

4	tablespoons melted butter	¼	cup dark brown sugar
1	teaspoon Worcestershire sauce	½	teaspoon mustard
		1	cup chopped pecans

Combine cheese, onion, garlic and dill. Mold into desired shape and refrigerate. Combine topping ingredients in a saucepan and heat until sugar is melted. Allow to cool and spread over cheese mold. Serve with crackers, chips, or mini toast.

A pretty presentation for this cheese ball is to add some type of red fruit for the holidays.

Cheddar Raspberry Spread

2	(20 ounce) packages Cracker Barrel Vermont sharp white Cheddar	1	(10 ounce) jar seedless raspberry jam
1	cup real mayonnaise	1	(4 ounce) package almonds, toasted
3	green onions, chopped		

Grate cheese in large mixing bowl. Add mayonnaise and green onions and mix thoroughly. Spread cheese mixture on round platter and chill. Just before serving, spread raspberry jam on top of cheese and sprinkle with almonds. Serve with your favorite crackers.

Fiesta Cheesecake

1½ cups crushed tortilla chips
¼ cup butter, melted
1 (8 ounce) package cream cheese, softened
1 (3 ounce) package cream cheese, softened
2 large eggs
2½ cups shredded Monterey Jack and Cheddar cheese
1 (4 ounce) can chopped green chiles, drained
¼ teaspoon ground red pepper

1 (8 ounce) carton sour cream
½ cup chopped green peppers
½ cup chopped sweet yellow pepper
½ cup chopped red pepper
½ cup chopped green onions
1 medium tomato, chopped, seeded and drained
1 bunch fresh cilantro
2 tablespoons chopped ripe olives, optional
Tortilla chips

Combine chips and butter and press onto bottom of lightly greased 9 inch springform pan. Bake at 325 degrees for 15 minutes and cool for at least 10 minutes. Beat cream cheese at medium speed with an electric mixer until fluffy. Add eggs, one at a time, beating after each addition. Stir in shredded cheese, chiles, and ground red pepper. Drop by spoonfuls into prepared pan and spread evenly. Bake at 325 degrees for 30 minutes. Cool for 10 minutes. Gently run a knife around edge of pan to release sides; carefully remove and let cool completely. Spread sour cream evenly over top. Mix chopped peppers, green onions, tomato and cilantro and put mixture on top. Add olives if desired. Cover and chill until ready to serve. Serve with tortilla chips.

Cheese Bites

3 loaves very thin Pepperidge Farm white bread
1 pound butter (4 sticks)
4 (5 ounce) jars Kraft Old English cheese spread

1½ teaspoons Worcestershire sauce
1 teaspoon Tabasco sauce
1 teaspoon onion powder
   Cayenne pepper

Trim crusts from bread. Beat butter, cheese, Worcestershire sauce, Tabasco sauce and onion powder. Spread mixture over each slice of bread. Stack 3 pieces of bread on top of one another. Cut stacks into 4 squares. Spread mixture along sides of all squares. Place squares on sprayed cookie sheet. Bake at 350 degrees for 15 to 20 minutes.

These freeze well, but you must freeze prior to baking.

Tomato-Cheddar Spread

1 (10 ounce) can tomatoes with green chilies, drained
1 cup mayonnaise
1 teaspoon Worchershire sauce

½ teaspoon salt
2 (8 ounce) blocks sharp Cheddar cheese, shredded
1 (4 ounce) jar chopped pimentos, drained

Stir together first 4 ingredients. Add cheese and pimento, mixing well. Refrigerate before serving with favorite crackers.

It is not recommended that pre-shredded cheese be used. The spread forms and holds better when starting with block cheese, so it is worth the effort put into grating it!

Curried Chutney Dip

1	pineapple	¼	cup fresh cilantro finely
1	(8 ounce) package cream		chopped
	cheese, room temperature	1	tablespoon curry powder
1	jar mango chutney		Crackers

Cut pineapple in half lengthwise leaving half the crown attached. Scoop out meat from one half. Cut in fine pieces to total ½ cup. Save the rest for another use. Combine remaining ingredients with the ½ cup chopped pineapple and place in hollowed out pineapple shell. Put shell on serving platter and serve with crackers.

Swiss Almond Dip

½	cup sliced almonds	¼	cup chopped green onion
2	(8 ounce) packages cream	2	dashes nutmeg
	cheese, room temperature		Pepper to taste
⅔	cup mayonnaise	3	slices fried bacon as garnish
3	cups shredded Swiss cheese		

Preheat oven to 350 degrees. In a dry frying pan over medium heat, toast the almonds until golden, shaking pan constantly to keep almonds moving, about 3 minutes. Remove from heat.

In a mixing bowl, beat together the cream cheese and mayonnaise until smooth. Stir in Swiss cheese, green onion and almonds. Season with nutmeg and pepper. Spread into a 1 quart baking dish or a 9 inch pie plate.

Bake for 20 minutes until slightly brown on top. Sprinkle with cooked bacon just before serving.

This is a great dip to serve with crackers, apple slices or bread slices.

Chutney is a condiment generally made with fruit and / or vegetables, vinegar, herbs and spices that provides a sweet and sour taste with flavors ranging from mild to very hot and spicy.

BLT Dip

12-14	slices cooked bacon, crumbled		Salt and pepper
1	(8 ounce) package cream cheese, softened		Shredded lettuce
1	cup mayonnaise	2	tomatoes, diced, drained and seeded

Combine first 3 ingredients. Add salt and pepper to taste. In the center of a serving plate set mixture in a mound. Surround the mound with shredded lettuce and pour diced tomatoes over the top of mound. Serve with Fritos, toast points or Melba toast crackers. Can be made ahead and refrigerated overnight.

Cucumber Dip

2	cucumbers, peeled and sliced into bite size pieces	¼	cup water
1	onion, cut into bite size pieces	4	tablespoons sugar
			Salt and pepper to taste
¾	cup vinegar	½	cup mayonnaise
		½	cup sour cream

Marinate cucumbers and onions in vinegar, water, salt and pepper in refrigerator overnight. Drain very well. Season with salt and pepper. Mix in mayonnaise and sour cream. Chill 2 to 3 hours.

The secret to this recipe is draining the cucumbers and onions very, very well. Serves best with crackers or Frito scoops.

Santa Fe Guacamole

2   avocados, mashed
2   tablespoons diced tomatoes
2   tablespoons diced onion
2   teaspoons diced jalapeño,
      seeds removed

1   tablespoon chopped cilantro
1   teaspoon minced, fresh garlic
½   lime, squeezed
      Salt and pepper to taste
      Tortilla chips

Mix all ingredients well and serve with chips.

This recipe is truly from Santa Fe, New Mexico. Friends visiting friends at a superb restaurant yielded in the kind waiter sharing this appetizer.

Bruschetta

2   large tomatoes, chopped
1   clove garlic, minced
6-8 basil leaves, slivered, plus a
      few more for garnish
2   tablespoons extra virgin
      olive oil
1   tablespoon balsamic vinegar

½   teaspoon kosher salt
      (or to taste)
½   teaspoon garlic salt
      (or to taste)
½   teaspoon garlic powder
      (or to taste)
1   baguette, sliced thinly on the
      diagonal

Combine all ingredients except the bread. Put olive oil on bread and broil until brown. Repeat for other side. Serve tomato mixture over the bread garnished with basil.

Stuffed Mushroom Caps

5	tablespoons margarine	3	tablespoons shredded Cheddar cheese
10	medium mushrooms, stems removed	2	tablespoons white wine
1	clove garlic, minced	1	teaspoon soy sauce
		⅓	cup round buttery crackers

Melt margarine in medium sized bowl and dip each mushroom in it. Place on baking sheet. In remaining margarine, mix garlic and cheese until well blended. Stir in wine, soy sauce and cracker crumbs. Mound the filling into each mushroom cap, pressing lightly. Broil 6 inches below broiler until filling is bubbly and lightly browned. Approximately 3 minutes. Serve warm.

The best thing about these scrumptious bites is that they can be made ahead and stored in the refrigerator prior to broiling.

South Georgia Vidalia Onion Dip

2	cups finely chopped Vidalia onions	1	cup mayonnaise
2	cups grated Swiss or Gruyère cheese	1	(8 ounce) package cream cheese
			Crackers or toast points

Mix all ingredients and spread in shallow dish. Bake at 325 degrees for 20 minutes.

Garden Fresh Salsa

2-3 tomatoes (preferably 2 large red and 1 yellow), chopped
2 tablespoons extra-virgin olive oil
1 teaspoon kosher salt (or to taste)
½ teaspoon red pepper flakes (or to taste)
Juice of 1 lime
1 small onion, chopped
½ bunch cilantro
1 fresh jalapeño, seeds removed, minced
20 slices jalapeños (from a jar)
⅓ cup jalapeño juice (from the jar)
1 teaspoon sugar
1 tablespoon cumin
Tortilla chips

Combine all of the above and serve with tortilla chips.

Chicken Wrap

½ cup red bell pepper, chopped
½ cup fresh broccoli, chopped
¼ cup water chestnuts, drained and chopped
2 tablespoons chopped onion
1 (5 ounce) can chunk chicken, drained and flaked
⅔ cup canned, condensed cream of chicken soup
1 cup shredded Colby-Jack cheese
2 (8 ounce) cans refrigerated crescent rolls
Paprika

Preheat oven to 350 degrees. Combine all ingredients except paprika and rolls. Unroll crescent rolls and arrange triangles in a circle on a round baking sheet, making sure to overlap flat edge to make a center circle and have the points outward. Scoop filling mixture onto widest portion of each triangle. Fold. Bake 25 to 30 minutes or until golden brown. Cut in pie pieces and serve warm.

Salsa in a Pinch

2   (28 ounce) cans diced
    tomatoes
6   green onions, chopped
1   bunch cilantro

1   lime
1   tablespoon minced garlic
    Salt and pepper

Drain tomatoes and pour into large bowl. Add onions. Chop cilantro, discarding stems. Roll lime on counter to bring juices to the surface, then cut and squeeze into mixture. Add garlic and salt and pepper to taste.

To make this salsa hot, just add canned jalapeño peppers to taste.

Mini Tomato Sandwich

½   cup mayonnaise
1   (3 ounce) package cream
    cheese, softened
1   teaspoon fresh, chopped
    basil

    Salt and pepper to taste
4   small tomatoes, sliced
1   baguette, sliced thin
    Bacon

Stir mayonnaise, cream cheese, basil, salt and pepper together and chill well. Drain sliced tomatoes on paper towel for 5 minutes on each side. Spread mixture on bread slices, and then top each with a tomato slice. Sprinkle with additional salt and pepper and garnish with bacon.

Sun-Dried Tomato Dip

1	(8 ounce) package cream cheese, room temperature	2-3	green onions
1	cup sour cream	10-12	dashes hot sauce
1	cup mayonnaise	1	teaspoon kosher salt
1/3	cup sun-dried tomatoes (in oil)	1	teaspoon pepper to taste

Combine cream cheese, sour cream, mayonnaise in food processor until smooth. Add tomatoes and onions until blended. Add hot sauce, salt and pepper and mix together. Serve with pita chips or thin crackers.

Chicken Sesame Bacon Nuggets

2	large skinned and boned chicken breasts	2	tablespoons sesame oil
8	bacon slices, cut into thirds	1	teaspoon ground ginger
1/2	cup orange marmalade	1	garlic clove, minced
1/4	cup soy sauce		Vegetable cooking spray
			Toothpicks

Cut chicken breast into 4 (1 inch) cubes. Wrap each chicken cube with bacon, and secure with a wooden toothpick. Stir together orange marmalade, soy sauce, sesame oil, ground ginger, and minced garlic in a shallow dish or large zip-top freezer bag. Add bacon-wrapped chicken cubes to mixture. Cover or seal and chill 2 hours, turning occasionally. Coat a rack and broiler pan with cooking spray. Place chicken nuggets on rack in boiler pan and bake at 450 degrees for 10 minutes, turn over and bake for 10 more minutes. Makes 6 servings.

Tex-Mex Chicken Cups

1½ pounds boneless chicken breast	4 teaspoons chili powder
1 cup Hidden Valley Ranch salad dressing	2 teaspoons paprika
¼ teaspoon salt	1 package (24) wonton wrappers
¼ teaspoon pepper	Salsa
2 cups Mexican shredded cheese	Sour cream

Poach chicken and drain and shred. Mix with dressing and season with salt and pepper. Preheat oven to 350 degrees. Spray muffin pans with cooking spray and place a wonton wrapper in each pressing it down with a small shot glass. Bake for 2 to 3 minutes until lightly brown. Combine shredded cheese with chili powder and paprika. Spoon chicken mixture into each wonton wrapper. Sprinkle with cheese mixture. Return to oven and bake until cheese is melted (5 to 7 minutes). Serve with salsa and sour cream as toppings.

Easy Cheese Dip

1 pound sausage	1 (8 ounce) package cream cheese, softened
1 can tomatoes with diced green chilies	Tostitos or Fritos

Brown sausage. Mix with tomatoes and cream cheese. Microwave until creamy and hot. Serve with chips.

Serve this dip in a small crock pot to keep it warmed.

Sausage Cheese Dip

1 pound ground chuck
1 pound hot bulk sausage
4 tablespoons dried minced onion
1 tablespoon Worcestershire sauce
1 pound Velveeta cheese, cubed
1 (10 ounce) can tomatoes with diced green chiles
1 teaspoon garlic salt
2 tablespoons chili powder
1 tablespoon white vinegar
1 can cream of mushroom soup
   Tortilla chips

Brown ground chuck and sausage and drain off fat. Add onion and brown. Transfer to a large pot or crock pot. Add rest of ingredients and mix thoroughly. Simmer until cheese is melted. Serve with tortilla chips.

Karen Scarborough,
Owner/Chef
Thyme Away Bed and Breakfast

Sausage Pinwheels

2 cups biscuit mix
½ cup milk
¼ cup butter, melted
1 pound recipe roll sausage, cooked and crumbled

Preheat oven to 400 degrees. Combine biscuit mix, milk and butter in large bowl until blended. Refrigerate 30 minutes. Divide mixture into 2 portions. Roll out 1 onto floured surface to ⅛ inch thick rectangle. Spread with half the sausage. Roll lengthwise into long roll. Repeat with remaining dough and sausage. Place rolls in freezer until hard enough to cut easily. Cut rolls into thin slices, place on baking sheet and bake for 15 minutes.

Wonton Shells

1 pound sausage, cooked and drained	1 small can chopped black olives
1 cup shredded Cheddar cheese	1 cup ranch dressing
1 cup grated Monterey Jack cheese	1 package wonton shells

Mix all ingredients together. Place shells in muffin pans and bake at 350 degrees until lightly browned. Spoon mixture into shells and bake for an additional 10 minutes.

Portofino Dip

2 (8 ounce) packages cream cheese, softened	1 (14 ounce) can artichoke hearts, cut into chunks
¾ cup grated Swiss cheese	1 pound fresh crabmeat, chopped
¾ cup grated Parmesan cheese	Crackers
⅓ cup white wine	
Salt and pepper to taste	

Preheat oven to 350 degrees. Mix first 5 ingredients. Spray bottom of oven safe serving dish with cooking spray. Layer artichokes followed by crabmeat. Top with cream cheese mixture. Bake until bubbly and serve with crackers.

Mexican Tuna Dip

1	can white tuna, well drained	20-30	cilantro leaves, chopped
¼	cup sour cream	1	teaspoon ground white pepper
¼	cup mayonnaise		Tortillas
½	cup chopped onion		
3-4	jalapeño peppers, finely chopped		

In food processor, blend tuna, sour cream and mayonnaise until smooth. Add jalapeños, cilantro and pepper. Chill. Toast tortillas and break into bite-sized chips.

Salmon Torte

6	tablespoons mayonnaise	¼	cup chopped chives
¾	stick butter, melted	½	cup minced fresh dill, divided
8	hard-boiled eggs, chopped	1	(8 ounce) package cream cheese, softened
½	cup chopped celery	½	cup sour cream
⅓	cup chopped red onion	8	ounces cooked, fresh salmon filet, chopped
1½	tablespoons fresh lemon juice	¼	cup capers
	Salt and pepper		Crackers
¼	cup chopped green onions		

In a bowl, whisk together the mayonnaise and butter. Stir in eggs, celery, red onion, lemon juice and season to taste with salt and pepper. Spread mixture evenly in an oiled 9 inch springform pan. Sprinkle with green onions, chives and ¼ cup dill. In small bowl stir together cream cheese and sour cream. Drop dollops of this mixture in the pan and spread carefully to form and even topping. Chill torte, covered at least 8 hours and up to 24 hours. Just before serving, run a knife around the edge and remove sides. Transfer torte to a serving plate. Combine chopped salmon, capers and remaining dill and spread evenly over torte. Serve with crackers. Makes 16 servings.

Robert Standard, Owner/Chef Kazan

Mexican Shrimp Cocktail

¼	cup ketchup	½	cup chopped tomato
¼	cup lime juice	¼	cup chopped onion
1-2	teaspoons Tabasco sauce	¼	cup chopped cilantro
1	pound shrimp cooked and peeled	1	avocado, chopped

Combine all ingredients, except avocado. Toss to coat shrimp. Chill 2 to 4 hours. Add avocado just before serving.

This is a great filling for lettuce wraps, as part of a salad or served with crackers.

Shrimp Diablo

1	pound large shrimp	1	(4 ounce) package Monterey Jack cheese
1	pound bacon		Toothpicks
4	jalapeño peppers		

Peel shrimp leaving tails on. Devein and butterfly shrimp. Cut cheese into ¼ x ¼ x 1½ inch long pieces. Cut jalapeño peppers into thin long slivers. (Leave seeds of pepper in to increase spice.) Cut bacon slices in half. (To avoid flame up when grilling, you may want to pre cook the bacon slightly in oven on a flat cookie sheet. Bacon should be raw and still flexible when removed from oven.)

Place 1 piece of cheese and 1 jalapeño pepper into the butterflied section of the shrimp and wrap entire shrimp with bacon. Secure with toothpick. Grill over medium heat and use soaked wood chips for added flavor. Serve hot off the grill or at room temperature.

Shrimp Pizza

2	(8 ounce) packages cream cheese	3-4	green onions, chopped
1	bottle Heinz cocktail sauce	1	small can black olives, drained
½	cup horseradish, or to taste	1	pound chopped, boiled shrimp
2	cups pizza blend shredded cheese		Cracker of choice

Spread cream cheese on large platter. Mix cocktail sauce and horseradish and spread over cream cheese. Layer shredded cheese, onions, olives and shrimp. Serve with crackers.

If you don't like such a hot taste, leave out the horseradish.

Party Mix

12	tablespoons butter	1	cup Wheat Chex cereal
4	tablespoons Dale's Seasoning Sauce (or regular Worcestershire sauce)	1	cup pretzels
		1	cup garlic flavored bagel chips broken in bite-sized pieces
3	teaspoons seasoned salt (Lowery's)	1	cup Goldfish snacks
2	teaspoons garlic powder	1	cup Fritos
1	teaspoon onion powder	1	cup Cheerios
2	cups Corn Chex cereal	1	cup Cheese-Its
2	cups Rice Chex cereal	1	small can mixed nuts

Heat oven to 250 degrees. Melt butter in large roasting pan in oven. Stir in seasonings and gradually stir in remaining ingredients until evenly coated.

Bake 1 hour stirring every 15 minutes. Let cool and store in airtight container.

Mustard Dip

1   cup dry mustard
²/₃ cup cider vinegar
¹/₃ cup white vinegar

1   cup sugar
2   eggs
¹/₂ teaspoon salt

Mix mustards and vinegar, let set overnight. Blend sugar, eggs and salt. Stir into mustard and cook over low heat until mixture thickens. Cool. Serve with pretzels, cheese or ham cubes.

Apple Dip

1   (8 ounce) package cream
    cheese
¹/₂ cup sugar
³/₄ cup light brown sugar

1   teaspoon vanilla extract
1   (6 ounce) package Heath
    Almond Brickle chips
    Sliced apples

Mix all the ingredients and serve with apples.

Cranberry Spread

1   (8 ounce) package cream
    cheese, softened
¹/₂ cup fresh, chopped
    cranberries

¹/₂ cup finely chopped pecans
2   tablespoons orange juice
¹/₄ teaspoon cinnamon

Blend all ingredients. Chill and serve with crackers of choice.

Pink Lemonade-Lime Dip

1   (14 ounce) can sweetened   1   (6 ounce) can frozen pink
     condensed milk   lemonade concentrate,
                                             thawed
                                       1   teaspoon grated lime rind

Stir together all ingredients in a small bowl until blended.

Cover and chill at least 2 hours.

Serve this tart dip with fresh fruit for a healthy snack or with sugar cookies for an easy dessert.

Sugar and Spice Pecans

1   egg white   ¼   teaspoon salt
1   tablespoon water   1   teaspoon cinnamon
1   cup sugar   1   pound pecans

Beat egg white and water until frothy (not stiff). Stir in sugar, salt, and cinnamon. Mix well. Add pecans and mix well until pecans are completely coated. Spread nuts thinly onto a large baking sheet. Bake at 200 degrees for 45 minutes, stirring every 15 minutes. Remove from oven when pecans are dry and toasty. When cool, store in airtight container.

Salads

GOOD WORKS
LAGRANGE WOMEN LEND A HELPING HAND

The women of LaGrange have always been quick to lend a hand to those in need. Perhaps none more than Viola Burks, one of Troup County's first social workers. A beloved, civic-minded educator, Viola served as the executive secretary of the LaGrange Welfare Association, which is now the United Way. She pioneered activities for needy children, helping endow a summer camp for children who otherwise would not have such an opportunity. Viola also served as the first director of the local chapter of the American Red Cross, established in 1917. Camp Viola, as it was later named, still exists today and is run by the Troup County Department of Recreation.

A group of LaGrange women also offered their services overseas. Jeanette Wilhoite, Teresa Antoinette "Nettie" Ward and Daisy Jackson drove ambulances in France during World War I. As members of the Ambulance Corps, they rescued wounded soldiers from the battlefront and drove them to the hospital. After returning to LaGrange, they continued their good works. Working with the Woman's Club and Rotary Club, Jeanette went on to establish the basis of what is now LaGrange Memorial Library. Whether at home or abroad, many LaGrange women throughout history possessed a philanthropic goodwill that continues on in the hearts of many local women today.

Salads

Salad Dressings

Antipasto Pasta Salad

PASTA

Salt
½ pound seashell pasta
2 ounces Genoa salami, chopped
2 ounces pepperoni sausage, chopped
¼ pound Asiago cheese, diced

1 (6 ounce) can black olives, drained and chopped
½ red bell pepper, diced
½ green bell pepper, diced
1½ tomatoes, chopped
1 (7 ounce) package dry Italian salad dressing mix

DRESSING

¼ cup plus 2 tablespoons extra virgin olive oil
2 tablespoons balsamic vinegar

1 tablespoon dried oregano
1½ teaspoons dried parsley
1½ teaspoons grated Parmesan cheese

In a large pot add salt to boiling water and cook pasta until al dente. Drain and cool by running under cold water. In a large bowl, combine everything except the dressing mix. Stir in the envelope of dressing mix last. Cover and refrigerate for at least 1 hour.

For the dressing, whisk together all ingredients. Just before serving, pour over the salad and mix well. Serves approximately 6.

Provolone cheese may be substituted for the Asiago.

Curry and Pine Nut Pasta Salad

1 clove garlic, cut into cubes	½ cup olive oil
1 teaspoon kosher salt	1 pound penne, cooked and drained
1 cup packed fresh basil	1 red onion, finely chopped
¼ cup lemon juice	⅔ cup pine nuts
¼ cup red wine vinegar	⅔ cup dried currants or dried cherries
1 teaspoon sugar	1 cup sliced black olives
1 teaspoon curry powder	
¼ teaspoon ground cumin	
½ teaspoon freshly ground black pepper	

Combine garlic, salt and basil in food processor and process until minced. Add lemon juice, vinegar, sugar, curry, cumin and pepper. Add olive oil gradually as processor is running.

Pour dressing over pasta in large bowl. Add onion, pine nuts, currants and olives and toss well. Season with additional pepper if desired. Chill, covered, for 2 hours or longer.

Kerri Vice, Owner/Chef Table Toppers Catering Co.

This salad can be enjoyed as this chef likes, warm, or as the recipe calls for, chilled. It can be prepared up to 1 day ahead.

Pasta Salad

4	cups mayonnaise	½	cup sugar
¾	cup sour cream	1	lemon, squeezed
2	tablespoons Dijon mustard	2	tablespoons pepper
3	tablespoons red wine vinegar	1	tablespoon salt
4	tablespoons malt vinegar	1	tablespoon oregano
3	tablespoons Worcestershire sauce	4	cups buttermilk
		3	pounds penne pasta, cooked

Mix all ingredients with penne pasta.

Tulla White, Owner/Chef The Basil Leaf, Venucci, Tulla's Bayou Bar and Grill and Tulla White Cuisine and Catering.

Lebanese Bread Salad (Fatoosh)

½	loaf Arabic Bread	4-5	leaves Romaine lettuce or ¼ head lettuce
1	small garlic clove		
	Salt and pepper to taste	1	cucumber, peeled and quartered
½	cup lemon juice		
½	cup parsley	2-3	medium tomatoes, cut into 1 inch cubes
3	green onions		
1	cup fresh mint or ¼ cup dried mint	½	cup olive oil

Toast bread to a golden brown and break into 1½ inch pieces. Set aside. In a salad bowl, mash the garlic, and mix well with salt and pepper. Add lemon juice to the garlic mixture and blend well. Coarsely chop the parsley, green onions, mint, cucumber, tomatoes, and toasted bread and add to the lemon and garlic mixture and toss thoroughly. Just before serving, add the olive oil and toss well. Makes 6 servings.

Chicken, Cheese and Artichoke Salad

3	cups diced cooked chicken	1	(14 ounce) can artichoke hearts, drained and diced
2	(8 ounce) packages cream cheese, softened	1	cup finely chopped pecans
2	cups shredded Parmesan cheese	4	green onions, minced
		1	tablespoon lemon juice
		½	teaspoon salt and pepper

Stir all ingredients together and chill for 8 hours.

Chutney Chicken Salad with Curry

2	cups, cooked, cubed chicken	2	tablespoons curry powder, or to taste
½	cup mayonnaise		Salt to taste
½	cup red raisins	1	cup dry roasted peanuts
½	jar (plus enough to garnish) Major Grey's Chutney	½	cup shredded coconut
4	green onions, chopped		Large lettuce leaves
4	eggs, hard-boiled and chopped		

Combine the first 8 ingredients. Stir well. Refrigerate 4 to 6 hours. Taste for curry flavor. Serve salad on lettuce leaves. Garnish with a tablespoon of Chutney. Sprinkle with peanuts and coconut. Makes 4 to 6 servings.

This recipe doubles well and is excellent served with warm croissants.

Quick-Fried Chicken Salad

¾ cup all-purpose flour
4 tablespoons snipped fresh basil
1 tablespoon finely shredded lemon peel
1 pound skinless boneless chicken breast strips
2 eggs beaten
2 tablespoons olive oil

4 cups mixed spring salad greens
1 head radicchio cut into bite-size pieces
2 cups sliced fresh strawberries
½ cup bottled balsamic vinaigrette salad dressing
4-6 Bibb or butter head lettuce leaves
¼ cup sunflower seeds, pecans, or walnuts, optional

In a shallow dish combine the flour, 2 tablespoon of basil and the lemon peel. Place eggs in another shallow dish. Dip chicken into flour mixture, then into the eggs and then again into flour mixture to coat. In a heavy skillet. Cook in oil, uncovered, for 6 to 8 minutes or until chicken is no longer pink, turning once. (If necessary, reduce heat to medium to prevent over browning and add more oil as needed during cooking.) Cool slightly. In a bowl, mix greens, radicchio and salad dressing. For each serving, place a Bibb leaf on a plate, top with greens mixture, strawberries and a couple of chicken strips. And nuts, if desired. Serve at room temperature. Makes 4 to 6 servings.

Any dressing of your choice works well with this salad.

Honey Chicken Salad

4 cups cooked chicken, chopped
3 celery ribs, diced
1 cup Craisins
½ cup toasted pecans, chopped

1½ cups mayonnaise
⅓ cup orange blossom honey
¼ teaspoon salt
¼ teaspoon pepper

Stir together the chicken, celery, Craisins and pecans. Whisk together the next 4 ingredients. Add to chicken mixture, stirring gently. Garnish with extra toasted pecans, if desired.

Curried Chicken and Rice Salad

4	chicken breast halves, skinned	¾	cup mayonnaise
½	teaspoon salt	1	teaspoon curry powder
1½	cups cooked rice	½	teaspoon salt
1	cup chopped celery	¼	teaspoon pepper
1	cup seedless grapes, halved		Lettuce leaves
½	cup chopped pecans, toasted	1	pint fresh strawberries, sliced
⅓	cup sweet pickle relish	1	fresh pineapple, peeled and cut into squares

Combine chicken and salt in Dutch oven. Add water to cover. Bring to a boil. Cover, reduce heat and simmer 40 minutes or until tender. Drain. De-bone chicken and cut into bite size pieces. Combine chicken, rice, and next 4 ingredients. Separately, combine mayonnaise and next 3 ingredients. Add chicken mixture, stirring well. Serve on lettuce leaves with strawberries and pineapple. Makes 4 to 6 servings.

Cucumber-Tomato Salad à la Eatzi's

2	large tomatoes, diced	½	teaspoon freshly ground pepper
2	cucumbers, peeled and diced	½	cup extra virgin olive oil
3	tablespoons red wine vinegar	1	cup fresh torn dill
1	small red onion, thinly sliced		
1	teaspoon kosher salt		

Combine the above ingredients. Serves 4 to 6.

For a variation, try 1 cup of fresh slivered basil instead of the dill.

45

Crunchy Cole Slaw

DRESSING

1 cup oil	2 packages seasoning from
½ cup sugar	beef flavor ramen noodles
⅓ cup white vinegar	

SALAD

2 packages oriental flavor	1 cup slivered almonds,
ramen noodles, crumbled	roasted
1 pound cole slaw mix	2 carrots, peeled and grated
1 cup sunflower seeds	1 bunch green onions, optional

Prepare dressing the night before. Break ramen noodles into small pieces. Add remaining ingredients. Mix with dressing and serve. Makes 10 to 12 servings.

Sweet and Sour Slaw

SLAW

1 head cabbage, chopped	1 green bell pepper, finely
1 medium onion, finely	chopped
chopped	½ cup finely chopped celery

DRESSING

1 cup sugar	1 teaspoon salt
¾ cup cider vinegar	½ teaspoon pepper
½ cup oil	¼ teaspoon celery seed

Combine cabbage, onion, green pepper and celery in large bowl and mix well. Combine dressing ingredients in a heavy saucepan. Bring to a boil over medium heat. Remove from heat and pour over cabbage mixture while still hot. Chill overnight. Makes 6 to 8 servings.

Using half white and half red cabbage makes for a pretty presentation.

Olive Salad

1 gallon large pimento stuffed green olives, slightly crushed and well drained
1 quart jar pickled cauliflower, drained and sliced
2 small jars capers, drained
1 whole stalk celery, sliced diagonally
4 large carrots, peeled and thinly sliced diagonally
1 small jar celery seeds
1 small jar oregano

1 large head fresh garlic, peeled and minced
1 teaspoon freshly ground pepper
1 jar pepperoncini, drained (left whole)
1 pound large Greek black olives
1 jar cocktail onions, drained
Olive oil
Vegetable oil

Combine all ingredients in a large bowl or pot and mix well. Place in a large jar and cover with ½ olive oil and ½ vegetable oil. Store tightly covered in refrigerator. Allow to marinate for at least 24 hours before using.

Makes a large portion, so consider giving it as a gift in smaller jars.

Cornbread Salad

SALAD

1 box Jiffy cornbread
1 bell pepper, chopped
1 purple onion, chopped
1 can pinto beans, drained

1 pound bacon, cooked and crumbled
3 dill pickles, chopped
3 tomatoes, chopped and drained

DRESSING

1 cup mayonnaise
1/2 cup dill pickle juice
1 tablespoon sugar

2 cups grated sharp Cheddar cheese

Prepare cornbread as directions note on back of box and crumble. Layer all ingredients in order in a 9 x 13 inch dish. To make dressing, mix mayonnaise, juice and sugar together. Cover salad with the dressing. Top with Cheddar cheese. Refrigerate 4 hours before serving.

Roasted New Potato Salad

2 tablespoons olive oil
2 pounds small red potatoes, diced
1/2 medium sweet onion, chopped
2 teaspoons minced garlic
1 teaspoon coarse salt
1/2 teaspoon freshly ground pepper

8-10 bacon slices, cooked and crumbled
1 bunch green onions, chopped
3/4 cup prepared Ranch dressing
Salt and pepper to taste

Preheat oven to 425 degrees. Place olive oil in 15 x 10 inch jelly-roll pan; add potatoes and next 4 ingredients, tossing to coat. Arrange potato mixture in a single layer. Stirring occasionally, bake for 30 to 35 minutes or until potatoes are tender. Transfer to a large bowl and toss with remaining ingredients. Serve immediately or cover and chill until ready to serve. Serves 4 to 6.

Marinated Sweet-n-Sour Salad

DRESSING

¼ **cup oil**
½ **cup white vinegar**

¾ **cup sugar**
Salt and pepper to taste

SALAD

1 **small can green peas,**
   drained
1 **can French green beans,**
   drained
1 **small jar chopped pimentos,**
   drained

1 **green pepper, hand-chopped**
1 **small onion, hand-chopped**
5-6 **stalks celery, hand-chopped**
1 **garlic clove, minced**

Mix oil, vinegar, sugar, salt and pepper together in a jar. Shake well. In a medium-sized bowl mix all other ingredients. Pour dressing over vegetables and cover. Refrigerate for at least 12 hours before serving.

This dish will keep for several weeks if refrigerated.

Dilled Potato Salad

4 **cups cold, diced potatoes**
¼ **cup vegetable oil**
2 **tablespoons fresh lemon**
   juice
2 **tablespoons instant minced**
   onions

1½ **teaspoons salt**
½ **teaspoon dill weed**
   Black pepper
⅛ **teaspoon garlic powder**
2 **tablespoons mayonnaise**
2 **tablespoons sour cream**

Mix first 8 ingredients, and marinate at least 1 hour. Just before serving, add the mayonnaise and the sour cream. Mix well. Makes 6 servings.

If you're looking for color during the winter holiday season, this is your dish! Add hot ham, biscuits, shrimp and grits and you've got the perfect dinner for friends.

Amelia Island Fruit Salad

SALAD

1	quart fresh strawberries	1	(11 ounce) can Mandarin
½	cup fresh blueberries		oranges
3	kiwis, peeled	⅛	cup toasted almonds
			Boston lettuce

DRESSING

⅛	cup sugar	1	teaspoon celery seed
1	teaspoon dry mustard	⅓	cup vinegar
1	teaspoon salt	1	cup vegetable oil
1	teaspoon paprika	1	tablespoon grated onion

Slice strawberries and kiwis. Mix all fruit together.

Whisk together all ingredients for dressing and chill. Serve fruit on Boston lettuce. Sprinkle with dressing and top with almonds.

Mixed Greens with Pecans, Goat Cheese and Dried Cranberries

¼	cup red wine vinegar	1½	cups dried cranberries
1	tablespoon Dijon mustard		(about 7 ounces)
1	tablespoon chopped fresh thyme	1	small red onion, thinly sliced
¾	cup olive oil	1½	cups glazed or honey-roasted pecans or walnuts
	Salt and pepper to taste	1	(5½ ounce) log soft fresh
2	(5 ounce) bags mixed baby greens		goat cheese, crumbled (about 1¼ cups)

Whisk vinegar, mustard, and thyme in small bowl. Gradually whisk in oil. Season dressing with salt and pepper. Mix greens, cranberries, and onion in large bowl. Mix in enough dressing to coat. Sprinkle with nuts and cheese. Makes 10 servings.

Autumn Salad

PECANS

2	tablespoons butter	4	dashes hot pepper sauce
¼	cup Worcestershire sauce	4	cups pecan halves
1	tablespoon ketchup		Salt

SALAD

1	bunch mixed greens	2	pears thinly sliced
3	green onions thinly sliced	½	cup crumbled blue cheese

DRESSING

2	tablespoons cider vinegar	Salt and pepper to taste
2	tablespoons olive oil	

Melt butter in large saucepan. Blend in Worcestershire sauce, ketchup and hot pepper sauce. Add pecans, stirring to coat thoroughly with sauce. Spread pecans evenly in a 13 x 9 x 2 inch baking pan. Bake at 400 degrees for 20 minutes stirring frequently to avoid burning. Spoon pecans on paper towels and sprinkle with salt. Mix salad ingredients together in bowl. Toss well and arrange on 4 salad plates. Top with pecans. Combine dressing ingredients in a jar, shake well and pour on salad.

Mandarin Tossed Greens

DRESSING

4 teaspoons chopped onion
1 cup apple cider vinegar
½ cup sugar

2 teaspoons dry mustard
2 teaspoons salt
1⅓ cups olive oil

SALAD

2 (10 ounce) bags spinach leaves
1 (10 ounce) bag spring greens
1 head iceberg lettuce
1 pound bacon, cooked and crumbled

2 red onions, finely sliced
8 ounces sliced portobello mushrooms
8 ounces sliced white mushrooms
3 cups Mandarin orange sections

Make dressing first. Combine onion, vinegar, sugar, dry mustard and salt in blender. Blend on low speed, slowly adding oil. Store in the refrigerator in blender canister.

To make the salad, mix and toss everything but the orange sections in a large bowl. Add the orange sections just before serving to prevent sogginess. Blend the dressing before tossing with the salad and serving. Serves 16 to 20.

Romaine and Strawberry Salad

SALAD
- 1 large head Romaine lettuce
- 1 large head Boston or butter lettuce
- 1 pint strawberries, slice
- 1 cup shredded Monterey Jack cheese
- ½ cup toasted walnuts

DRESSING
- 1 cup vegetable oil
- ¾ cup sugar
- ½ cup red wine vinegar
- 2 garlic cloves, minced
- ½ teaspoon salt
- ½ teaspoon paprika
- ¼ teaspoon white pepper

Tear all lettuce into bite-sized pieces. Combine them with strawberries, cheese and walnuts. For dressing: combine all ingredients in large jar, cover and shake. Before serving, shake dressing and pour over salad.

Grape Salad

- 1 (8 ounce) package cream cheese, softened
- 1 (8 ounce) carton sour cream
- ½ cup sugar
- 2-3 cups red seedless grapes
- 1 teaspoon vanilla extract
- ½ cup brown sugar
- 1 cup chopped pecans

Mix cream cheese, sour cream, sugar and vanilla extract together well. Fold in grapes, and spread in medium sized serving dish. On top of mixture, spread brown sugar and then the pecans. Refrigerate for 8 hours or overnight. Serves approximately 10.

This dish has been known to incite bribing over the last serving. It's mainly used as a refreshing summer dessert or accompaniment to dinner.

Poppy Seed Craisin Salad

SALAD

1 bag salad greens	1 pear, cut into bite-sized pieces
1 small carton plain feta cheese	1 green apple, cut into bite-sized pieces
1 small bag chopped walnuts	½ small package real bacon pieces
1 package Craisins	

DRESSING

½ cup sugar	⅓ cup apple cider vinegar
1 teaspoon salt	1 tablespoon lemon juice
1 teaspoon dry mustard	1 cup vegetable oil
½ teaspoon onion powder	1½ tablespoons poppy seeds

Toss all salad ingredients together. For dressing, combine sugar, salt, dry mustard, onion powder, vinegar and lemon juice. Stir until sugar dissolves. Add oil slowly, mixing well. Dressing will thicken as oil is added. Stir in poppy seeds. Store in refrigerator until ready to serve. Shake dressing well before serving with salad. Serves 8 to 10.

As it is somewhat sweet, this dressing is also really good on a fruit or avocado salad.

Spinach Strawberry Salad

SALAD

Spinach leaves
Green leaf lettuce
Mushrooms, sliced

Strawberries, sliced
Walnuts, chopped

DRESSING

½ **cup sugar**
2 **tablespoons sesame seeds**
1 **tablespoon poppy seeds**
1½ **teaspoons minced onion**

¼ **teaspoon Worcestershire sauce**
½ **cup vegetable oil**
¼ **cup apple cider vinegar**

Mix salad ingredients. Mix dressing ingredients. Pour dressing over salad and serve.

Strawberry Fields

SALAD

2 **bags pre-washed spring mix salad greens**
10 **strawberries, sliced**

1 **(8 ounce) package crumbled feta cheese**

DRESSING

½ **cup vegetable oil**
½ **cup red wine vinegar**

½ **cup sugar**
1 **tablespoon dry mustard**

Put salad greens in large bowl with the sliced strawberries and feta cheese on top. Mix all dressing ingredients together in a separate bowl and pour over salad. Toss gently and serve immediately.

Blush Vinaigrette Dressing

⅓	cup sugar	¼	teaspoon Worcestershire sauce
2	teaspoons minced onion	½	cup red wine vinegar
1	tablespoon poppy seeds	1	cup canola oil

Combine all ingredients but the oil. Gradually whisk in oil.

If you mix this dressing in a blender, it will turn out creamier.

Creamy Vinaigrette Dressing

3	tablespoons tarragon vinegar	1	tablespoon mayonnaise
½	cup extra-virgin olive oil	½	teaspoon freshly ground pepper
¾	teaspoon kosher salt	⅛	teaspoon garlic powder
1	teaspoon Dijon mustard		

Combine all the ingredients and shake until well mixed.

French Russian Dressing

½	cup vinegar	¾	cup sugar
2	teaspoons salt	⅓	cup catsup
1	cup vegetable oil		

Combine all ingredients. Whisk then shake until well combined.

Served best on a spinach salad.

56

Classic Blue Cheese Dressing

1	cup mayonnaise	1	tablespoon freshly squeezed lemon juice
½	cup crumbled blue cheese, divided	¼	teaspoon Worcestershire sauce
½	cup half-and-half	½	teaspoon kosher salt
1	tablespoon Dijon mustard		Freshly ground black pepper
2	tablespoons sour cream		
10	dashes Tabasco sauce		

Whisk mayonnaise, ¼ cup of the blue cheese, half-and-half, mustard, sour cream, Tabasco sauce, lemon juice and Worcestershire sauce together. Gently stir in remaining blue cheese and salt and pepper.

It's always better the next day!

Sweet Balsamic Vinegar Dressing

1	green onion	1	teaspoon salt
1	lemon	1	teaspoon celery seed
3	tablespoons sugar	¼	cup balsamic vinegar
1	tablespoon Dijon mustard	1	cup extra virgin olive oil

Chop green onion. Remove zest from lemon and squeeze lemon juice. In blender or food processor, combine all ingredients except the oil and blend until smooth. Transfer mixture to a bowl and whisk in oil. Serves 10.

Robert Standard, Owner/Chef Kazan

Simple and perfect for butter lettuce and fresh tomatoes.

White Balsamic Vinaigrette Dressing "Venucci Salad Dressing"

2	white onions, diced	2	tablespoons salt
6	cups white balsamic vinegar	2	tablespoons pepper
4	tablespoons garlic	2	cups honey
4	tablespoons parsley	3	tablespoons finely chopped,
16	ounces Parmesan cheese		fresh ginger
2	tablespoons Dijon	32	ounces blended oil
2	tablespoons oregano		

Combine all ingredients except oil and mix well. Slowly whisk in blended oil.

Tulla White, Owner/Chef The Basil Leaf, Venucci, Tulla's Bayou Bar and Grill and Tulla White Cuisine and Catering

Salads

GOOD WORKS

LAGRANGE WOMEN LEND A HELPING HAND

The women of LaGrange have always been quick to lend a hand to those in need. Perhaps none more than Viola Burks, one of Troup County's first social workers. A beloved, civic-minded educator, Viola served as the executive secretary of the LaGrange Welfare Association, which is now the United Way. She pioneered activities for needy children, helping endow a summer camp for children who otherwise would not have such an opportunity. Viola also served as the first director of the local chapter of the American Red Cross, established in 1917. Camp Viola, as it was later named, still exists today and is run by the Troup County Department of Recreation.

A group of LaGrange women also offered their services overseas. Jeanette Wilhoite, Teresa Antoinette "Nettie" Ward and Daisy Jackson drove ambulances in France during World War I. As members of the Ambulance Corps, they rescued wounded soldiers from the battlefront and drove them to the hospital. After returning to LaGrange, they continued their good works. Working with the Woman's Club and Rotary Club, Jeanette went on to establish the basis of what is now LaGrange Memorial Library. Whether at home or abroad, many LaGrange women throughout history possessed a philanthropic goodwill that continues on in the hearts of many local women today.

Soups and Sandwiches

PERSEVERANCE
WOMEN TURN PASSION INTO LIVELIHOOD

Many Troup County women have put their hearts and souls into the food they prepare and some have gone onto make that passion their livelihoods. They have often done so without any formal training, but with plenty of perseverance. In the late 1960s, Betty Daniel was one such woman. She started out opening an antique and gift shop in Handley's Old General Store, which had long been a part of the family's plantation. At that time, they also had a cotton gin, dairy and several slave cabins, which were later torn down. Their antebellum home and general store still stand near Interstate-85 in LaGrange.

Better later bought an additional old house, dating back to about 1860, that was previously used as a residence for employees of Callaway Mills. Soon after, Betty learned that Lafayette Parkway, a major thoroughfare, would be built where her house and many other old homes were standing. To save these lovely old buildings from the wrecking ball, Betty decided to move some of them to vacant land on Morgan Street. She moved St. John's Methodist Church, her big house, a smaller mill house and a house built with pegs, dating back to about 1840. In this location, she soon opened her restaurant, Taste of Lemon, serving traditional Southern food with a distinct flavor. Unfortunately, two of the homes were lost to a fire in 2005. However, that has not stopped Betty from keeping the doors of her restaurant open.

Betty says, "I started the restaurant because I couldn't find anyone else who was interested in opening a restaurant of the type that I had in mind. So, I jumped in with no experience – a foolish move when I look back on it now. However, we did survive, due to long hours and a lot of hard work. We are very grateful to our wonderful customers in LaGrange and from all around. It's so exciting when someone comes in from out of town and says someone told them to be sure and stop by Taste of Lemon in LaGrange for lunch."

Soups

Sandwiches

Beer Cheese Soup

1 tablespoon butter
½ cup chopped onion
½ teaspoon minced garlic
1 teaspoon Worcestershire
   sauce
1 (12 ounce) can beer

1 (14½ ounce) can chicken
   broth
3 tablespoons cornstarch
2 cups half-and-half
2 cups shredded sharp
   Cheddar cheese
   Bacon bits

Melt margarine in a 4½ quart pot over medium heat. Add onion, garlic and Worcestershire sauce and stir well. Add beer, raise heat and boil for 3 minutes to evaporate alcohol. Add chicken broth and bring back to a boil. Lower the heat to medium-low and simmer. In a separate bowl, combine the cornstarch with 3 tablespoons water and stir until smooth. Set aside. Add the half-and-half and cheese to the soup. Stir constantly until the cheese melts. Then stir in the cornstarch mixture. Stir constantly until the soup is thick, about 2 minutes. Serve garnished with bacon bits. Serves 6.

Spicy Cabbage-Beef Soup

2 pounds ground beef,
   browned and well drained
1 large onion, chopped
5 cups cabbage, cut into
   bite-sized pieces
2 (16 ounce) cans red kidney
   beans
3 (8 ounce) cans tomato sauce
2 cups water
1 green bell pepper, seeded
   and chopped

¾ cup picante sauce
4 beef bouillon cubes
1½ teaspoons ground cumin
1 teaspoon salt
½ teaspoon pepper
1 dash or 2 Everglades
   seasoning
1 dash or 2 Worcestershire
   sauce

Mix all ingredients in crock pot and cook on low for 8 to 10 hours.

Beef Goulash

½	cup vegetable oil	12	cups beef broth
6	ounces lean beef, cut into ¼ inch cubes	2	cups diced potato
		1	cup cubed red bell pepper
1	cup diced onion	1	cup cubed green bell pepper
2	garlic cloves, sliced	1	cup cubed yellow bell pepper
	Pinch caraway seeds	2	teaspoons lemon zest
2	tablespoons mild paprika	2	tablespoons lemon juice
4	tablespoons all-purpose flour		Salt and pepper

In large heavy sauce pot, heat oil over high heat. Add beef and sauté until lightly brown. Add onion and continue to sauté for 5 minutes, stirring often. Reduce heat to medium and add garlic, caraway and paprika. Continue cooking 3 minutes. Sprinkle in flour and stir, and then add beef broth. Turn heat up to high, bringing soup to a boil. Reduce heat and simmer for 10 minutes. Add potato and simmer 10 more minutes. Add peppers and continue cooking for 5 minutes or until potato is tender. Add lemon zest and juice. Season with salt and pepper. Serves 8.

Jamie Keating, Owner/Chef Gourmet Events

Corn and Bacon Chowder

3	slices bacon	1	(17 ounce) can cream style corn
2	cups milk		
1	envelope chicken noodle soup mix with diced white chicken meat	½	cup grated cheese

Microwave bacon on high 3 minutes, remove and crumble. Combine remaining ingredients, except cheese, in 3-quart casserole. Microwave uncovered 9 minutes, stirring twice. Stir in bacon and top with grated cheese. Serve with crusty bread and a tossed green salad. Serves 4.

Cilantro-Lime Soup

2	tablespoons olive oil	1	cup corn kernels
1	medium onion, chopped	1	cup peeled, seeded and diced tomato
2	cloves garlic, minced		
1	tablespoon chili powder	¼	cup chopped cilantro
2	skinless, boneless chicken breasts	¼	cup fresh lime juice
			Salt and pepper
5	cups chicken broth	8	teaspoons sour cream

Heat oil in heavy saucepan over medium-high heat. Add onion and garlic to sauté until slightly softened. Add chili powder and stir 1 minute. Cut chicken breasts into chunks and add to the pan, stirring 2 minutes. Add broth, corn and tomatoes. Bring to a boil. Reduce heat and simmer until chicken is cooked through, about 10 minutes. Add cilantro and lime juice. Season with salt and pepper. Garnish with sour cream. Serves 8.

Robert Standard, Owner/Chef Kazan

Split Pea Soup

2	tablespoons vegetable oil	1	(12 ounce) can beer
1	medium leek (white and green parts), rinsed and thinly sliced	10	leaves Boston Bibb lettuce, shredded
		2	bay leaves
2	medium carrots, sliced	5	fresh mint leaves, chopped or ½ teaspoon dry mint, crushed, optional
1	pound dried green split peas, rinsed and drained		
3	(14½ ounce) cans vegetable broth	1½	teaspoons liquid smoke
		½	cup sour cream

In a large saucepan, heat oil over medium heat. Add leek and carrots and cook, stirring occasionally, until leeks are very soft, about 10 minutes. Add split peas, broth, beer, lettuce, bay leaves, and mint, if desired. Bring to a boil, cover, and reduce heat to low. Cook until split peas soften to purée, about 1 to 1½ hours. Discard bay leaves and stir in liquid smoke. Serve hot with a dollop of sour cream.

Gazpacho

3	pounds diced ripe tomatoes	1	tablespoon chopped chives
2	medium diced cucumbers	3	tablespoons lemon juice
1	medium chopped onion	1	teaspoon paprika
2	crushed cloves garlic	½	cup olive oil
4	cups chilled tomato juice		Salt to taste
½	teaspoon dried basil		Pepper to taste
½	teaspoon dried tarragon		Hot sauce to taste
3	tablespoons chopped parsley		

Combine all ingredients into large bowl. Stir well. Chill. Serves 12.

Classic Minestrone

1	large leek, chopped	1	teaspoon chopped fresh thyme or ½ teaspoon dried
2	chopped carrots	1	(14 ounce) can cannelloni (white kidney beans) or kidney beans
1	zucchini, thinly sliced		
¾	cup whole green beans, halved	1	(2 ounce) bag small pasta shapes or macaroni
2	celery stalks, thinly sliced		Salt
3	tablespoons olive oil		Ground black pepper
6¼	cups stock (beef or vegetable)		Finely grated Parmesan cheese, to garnish, optional
1	(14 ounce) can chopped tomatoes		Fresh parsley, chopped, garnish
1	tablespoon chopped fresh basil		

Put all the fresh vegetables into a large saucepan with the olive oil. Heat until sizzling, then cover, lower the heat and sweat the vegetables for 15 minutes, shaking the pan occasionally. Add the stock, tomatoes, herbs and seasoning. Bring to a boil, replace the lid and simmer gently for about 30 minutes. Add the canned beans and their liquid together with the pasta, and simmer for 10 minutes more. Check the seasoning and serve hot, sprinkled with the Parmesan cheese, if using, and chopped fresh parsley. Serves 4.

Mama's Vegetable Soup

1	ham bone	1	(14 ounce) can green beans
1	pound hamburger or ground turkey	1	(8 ounce) can tomato sauce
2	(14 ounce) cans stewed tomatoes	3	cups diced potato
2	packages frozen chopped okra	3	cups sliced onion
1	(14 ounce) can kernel corn	1/2	head shredded cabbage
		1/2-3/4	cup ketchup to taste
		2	teaspoons garlic powder
			Pepper to taste

In large soup pot, cover ham bone with water. Bring to a boil, reduce heat to medium simmer. Cook until meat falls off bone. Cook hamburger in pan and drain off grease. Add to soup pot with stock. Add all remaining ingredients, except cabbage. Bring to boil and cook at medium-high 1 hour. Add cabbage, simmer at least 5 hours. Serves 18 to 20.

Crab and Pumpkin Bisque

2	tablespoons extra virgin olive oil	1	quart heavy cream
2	pounds pumpkin, freshly diced	1/4	teaspoon nutmeg
2	tablespoons chopped garlic	1 1/2	pounds pumpkin purée
1/3	cup chopped shallot	1	tablespoon honey
1 1/2	quarts chicken or seafood stock	7	ounces light brown sugar
			Kosher salt and white pepper
		1	pound lump crabmeat

Sauté first 4 ingredients in a large soup pot. Deglaze pan with the stock and simmer 20 minutes. Add cream, nutmeg and pumpkin purée. Finish the soup with honey and sugar. Adjust seasonings of salt and pepper as desired. Top with lump crabmeat.

Jamie Keating, Owner/Chef Gourmet Events

Potato Soup

5	pounds potatoes, peeled, cut, boiled and drained	1	medium onion, fried in bacon grease
2	cans cream of celery soup	1	stick melted butter
4	cans evaporated milk		Lemon pepper seasoning to taste
1	pound bacon, fried and drained		

Combine all ingredients and cook on low.

Lobster and Mushroom Bisque

½	pound green peppers, diced	1	cup fresh chopped parsley
1½	pounds Spanish onions, diced	¼	teaspoon Tabasco sauce or cayenne pepper
1	quart sliced fresh mushrooms	2	cups dry sherry
2	pounds lobster meat, cooked	1	gallon of milk or half-and-half
5	teaspoons salt	¾	pound butter
½	teaspoon white pepper	2½	cups all-purpose flour for roux
2	teaspoons paprika		

Sauté green peppers, onions and mushrooms in butter until golden. Slowly add flour, stirring constantly to form a roux. Simmer several minutes on low flame to set roux. Slowly whisk in warmed milk or half-and-half until roux is completely dissolved. While simmering and occasional stirring, add salt, pepper, paprika, parsley and Tabasco sauce. As temperature of bisque raises, it will thicken. Occasional stirring is important to prevent sticking. Add sherry and lobster meat after bisque has thickened fully. Cook for 10 minutes more, then remove from heat. Serve immediately with more chopped parsley and a shake of paprika as a garnish.

Shrimp and Crab Corn Chowder

2   sticks butter
1½ cups chopped spring onions
    with tops
3   tablespoons flour
1   quart half-and-half
1   (16 ounce) tube frozen cream
    corn
2   (21 ounce) cans cream of
    celery soup
1   (14 ounce) can clear chicken
    broth
2   (22 ounce) cans summer
    crisp whole kernel golden
    sweet corn

2   (12 ounce) cans lump
    crabmeat
1   (12 ounce) bag cooked,
    peeled, tailless small shrimp
1   (4 ounce) jar pimentos
¾   teaspoon garlic powder
1   teaspoon chili powder
    Salt and pepper
2   tablespoons sherry, optional
12 ounces crumbled bacon
2   cups sharp shredded cheese

In a large pot, prepare roux by melting butter and sautéing onion on medium-high until bulb is clear. Do not brown. Add flour and cook, stirring constantly, until mixture thickens. Gradually add half-and-half while stirring to ensure no lumps. Add remaining ingredients except sherry. Cover and heat thoroughly on medium, stirring often. Frozen corn will take a while to thaw. Allow to cook for at least 1 hour. Do not simmer. Add sherry right before serving. Garnish serving bowls with bacon and cheese. Serves at least 20.

This recipe is freezer friendly so even if you're not planning to serve 20, make the whole recipe so you'll have leftovers.

Shrimp and Spinach Chowder

4	cups chicken broth	8	cups spinach, stemmed and
½	cup grated yellow onion		sliced into ribbons
½	cup grated carrot	2	cups heavy cream
1	teaspoon salt	1	tablespoon lemon zest,
½	teaspoon pepper		minced
¼	teaspoon nutmeg	3	cups red potatoes, diced
6	tablespoons butter	½	pound medium shrimp,
6	tablespoons all-purpose flour		peeled and deveined
1	cup milk		Tabasco sauce to taste

Simmer broth with onion, carrot and potatoes for 15 minutes in soup pot. In small pan, melt butter and whisk in flour on low heat. Whisk in milk until smooth. Cook 2 minutes. Add to broth mixture. Stir in spinach and shrimp and cook to wilt (about 3 minutes). Cook shrimp through. Turn off heat, and stir in cream and Tabasco sauce.

Shrimp Primavera

2	tablespoons butter	1	pound package frozen
⅓	cup chopped green onions		vegetables with pasta
3	tablespoons flour		primavera style (garlic)
½	teaspoon thyme	1	can artichoke hearts
¼-½	teaspoon salt	½	pound cooked shrimp
¼	teaspoon cayenne pepper	1	cup whipping cream
2	(14½ ounce) cans chicken		Parmesan cheese
	broth		Green onions

Melt butter in large saucepan over medium heat. Add onions, cook until tender. Stir in flour, salt, thyme, cayenne pepper and ¼ cup chicken broth. Stir until smooth. Stir in remaining broth. Bring to boil. Stir in vegetables with pasta and artichoke hearts. Return to a boil. Reduce heat to low, simmer 3 to 5 minutes or until vegetables are tender crisp. Stir in shrimp and cream. Cook 2 to 3 minutes or until thoroughly heated, stirring occasionally. Do not boil. Top each serving of soup with 2 teaspoons Parmesan and 1 teaspoon green onions.

Basic Chili

1 pound mild sausage	1 (16 ounce) can dark red kidney beans, drained
1 pound ground beef	
1 medium onion, chopped	1 (16 ounce) can light red kidney beans, drained
1 small chopped green pepper	
1 small chopped red pepper	1 (16 ounce) can southwestern style black beans, drained
1 small chopped orange pepper	
	1 tablespoon chili powder
1 clove minced garlic	2 teaspoons ground cumin
1 (28 ounce) can diced tomatoes, undrained (I use the chili flavored.)	½ teaspoon salt
	½ teaspoon cayenne pepper
	1 cup water

Sauté sausage and ground beef in a large, heavy saucepan until browned, stirring to crumble sausage; drain excess grease and return to pan. Sauté onion, peppers and garlic in another pan until translucent. Combine all ingredients into the largest saucepan. Cover and simmer 1 to 1½ hours. This can also be done in a crockpot on low for several hours. Additional water may be added if needed. Serves 8.

Chicken Chili

4 boneless chicken breasts, cooked and shredded	½ onion, chopped
	1 (¼ cup) regular chili packet
1 (28 ounce) can crushed tomatoes	½ (⅛ cup) packet hot chili mix
	2 tablespoons sugar
1 (28 ounce) can water	1 tablespoon chili powder
2 cans regular chili beans	Salt to taste
1 can kidney beans	Pepper to taste
½ bell pepper, chopped	

Mix together crushed tomatoes, water, chili beans, kidney beans, bell pepper, onion, chili packets, sugar, chili powder. Add chicken. Season to taste. Simmer 2 to 3 hours. Serve with cheese, Fritos, and sour cream. Serves 10.

Hot Italian Chili

1	pound hot Italian sausage	2	(32 ounce) cans Italian plum tomatoes, drained
1	pound sweet Italian sausage	6	plum tomatoes, diced
	Olive oil	1	beer
2	cups coarsely chopped onion	1	cup red wine
6–10	cloves garlic, minced	1	cup chopped parsley
2	pounds fajita beef	1	can tomato paste
5	cans chili beans	6	teaspoons chili powder
2	green peppers, cored, seeded and chopped	3	teaspoons ground cumin
2	red peppers, cored, seeded and chopped	2	teaspoons dried oregano
6	fresh jalapeño peppers, cored, seed and diced to ⅛ inch	1	teaspoon dried basil
		2	teaspoons salt
		2	teaspoons fresh black pepper

Brown sausage and drain. In large stock pot, cook onions and garlic in olive oil until wilted. Add fajita beef and brown. Add sausages, bell peppers and jalapeño peppers and cook until peppers are slightly wilted. Remove from heat and add everything but fresh tomatoes. Return to heat and cook slowly for at least 10 minutes, adding tomatoes in last. Serve with sour cream, cheese and oyster crackers. Makes 8 to 10 servings or more.

Kerri Vice, Owner/Chef Table Toppers Catering Co.

Pepperoncini Rosso Italiano Di Stile (Italian Style Chili)

2 pounds sweet Italian sausage meat, casings removed and browned and drained

8 pounds ground beef chuck, browned and drained

½ cup best quality olive oil

1½ tablespoons freshly ground black pepper

3 tablespoons minced fresh garlic

4 ounces plain chili powder

4 tablespoons salt

6 pounds canned Italian plum tomatoes, drained

½ cup burgundy wine

½ cup fresh dill

2 teaspoons Tabasco sauce

3 (16 ounce) cans, dark red kidney beans, drained

4 (5 ounce) cans, pitted small black olives, drained

1¾ pounds yellow onions, coarsely chopped

1 (12 ounce) can tomato paste

3 ounces ground cumin seed

¼ cup prepared Dijon-style mustard

4 tablespoons dried basil

4 tablespoons dried oregano

¼ cup lemon juice

½ cup fresh Italian parsley

4 tablespoons ground jalapeños

Heat olive oil in a huge stock pot, add onion and sauté for about 10 minutes until translucent. Add the garlic, jalapeños, cumin, chili powder, and mustard and sauté for 10 minutes. Combine all ingredients into the huge crock pot and let stew for a few hours, stirring often. Serves 24.

Grilled Eggplant Sandwich

1	eggplant		1	loaf French or Italian bread
1	red or yellow bell pepper			Mozzarella cheese
4	slices Vidalia onion			Black pepper
1	clove crushed garlic			Sliced tomato, optional

Wash eggplant and slice into ¼ inch slices lengthwise. Seed and clean pepper. Season eggplant and bell pepper with garlic and pepper. Place eggplant, bell pepper, and Vidalia onion on grate of a very hot grill, sprayed with cooking spray. Cook with lid down until vegetables are brown on each side, approximately 10 minutes. Slice bread and assemble sandwiches. Makes 4 to 6 servings.

Pickled Okra Sandwiches

1	(24 ounce) loaf sliced white bread		1	(16 ounce) jar pickled okra
1	(8 ounce) package cream cheese, softened		1	cup finely chopped fresh parsley

Remove crust from bread. With rolling pin, roll slices very thin. Coat each slice with cream cheese and place an okra spear in center. Roll up. Spread a light coat of cream cheese on each rolled up sandwich. Roll sandwich in finely chopped parsley. Cut in half if desired.

Lettuce Wraps

SAUCE

½ cup apricot preserves	2 minced garlic cloves
⅓ cup fresh lime juice	1 teaspoon cornstarch
2 tablespoons soy sauce	

WRAPS

1 tablespoon dark sesame oil or vegetable oil	½ cup grated carrot
2 boneless, skinless chicken breasts, chopped in small pieces	2 tablespoons chopped peanuts
	1 teaspoon grated gingerroot
½ cup chopped seeded cucumber	1 teaspoon chopped garlic
	16 leaves (about 2 heads) butterhead (Bibb) lettuce

In a small bowl, combine preserves, lime juice, soy sauce and garlic. Mix well. Spoon ¼ cup sauce into 1 cup measuring cup. Stir in cornstarch until smooth. Set aside. Refrigerate remaining sauce in bowl until serving time. Heat oil in medium skillet over medium-high heat until hot. Add chicken. Cook 5 to 7 minutes or until browned, stirring frequently. Stir in cucumber, carrot, peanuts, gingerroot and garlic. Stir in reserved sauce with cornstarch. Cook 2 to 3 minutes or until bubbly and thick, stirring constantly. Spoon mixture into shallow dish. Cover and refrigerate 30 minutes or until cooled. Spoon 2 tablespoons chicken mixture onto center of each lettuce leaf. Fold sides of lettuce in toward center. Roll up like a burrito and secure with toothpicks. Serve immediately, or cover and refrigerate until serving time. Serve with remaining sauce. Makes 16 servings.

Mexican Veggie Roll-Ups

1   (3 ounce) package cream
      cheese, softened
1/3 cup sour cream
1   tablespoon taco seasoning
      mix
1/2 cup fresh corn kernels,
      cooked or frozen corn
      kernels, thawed and drained
1/2 cup canned black beans,
      drained

1/4 cup finely chopped fresh
      cilantro
1   Italian plum tomato, seeded
      and finely chopped
2   tablespoons thick and
      chunky-style salsa
3   (10-inch) garden spinach and
      vegetable, tomato or plain
      flour tortillas

In a small bowl combine cream cheese, sour cream and taco seasoning mix; beat until well blended. Stir in corn, beans, cilantro, tomato and salsa. Spread cream cheese mixture over each tortilla to the edges. Roll up each tortilla and cut off tapered ends. Wrap each tortilla roll in plastic wrap. Refrigerate at least 1 hour or up to 8 hours before serving. To serve, cut each roll into 1-inch slices. Makes 24 servings.

Italian Beef Sandwiches

Garlic salt
Crazy Gourmet salt
Fresh cracked peppercorns
Crushed oregano

1   (5-6 pound) eye of round
      roast
1/2 cup red wine
1/4 cup Worcestershire sauce
Variety of sandwich rolls

Sprinkle garlic salt, gourmet salt, pepper and oregano over all sides of the beef roast. Place in oven cooking bag. Pour the wine and Worcestershire sauce over the beef and seal the bag. Place the bag on a baking sheet. Bake at 250 degrees for 5 to 6 hours or 1 hour per pound. Let stand for 5 to 10 minutes. Slice and arrange on a serving platter. Drizzle with pan juices if desired. Serve with rolls, horseradish sauce and mustard, if desired.

73

French Dip Sandwiches

1	(3½-4 pound) boneless chuck roast, trimmed	1	teaspoon dried rosemary, crushed
½	cup soy sauce	1	teaspoon dried thyme
1	beef bouillon cube	1	teaspoon garlic powder
1	bay leaf	12	French sandwich rolls, split
3-4	peppercorns		

Place trimmed roast in 5-quart slow cooker. Combine soy sauce and next 6 ingredients; pour over roast. Add water to slow cooker until roast is almost covered. Cook covered on low for 7 hours or until very tender. Remove roast. Reserve broth and shred roast with a fork. Place roast in rolls, and serve with reserved broth for dipping.

Pepperoncini Beef Sandwiches

1	beef roast	**Crispy French rolls**
1	jar pepperoncini	

Place beef roast in crock pot. Add jar of pepperoncini, including the juice but minus the stems. Allow to cook all day. When done, shred the meat and return to slow cooker until serving time. Using a slotted ladle, serve on crispy French rolls.

Can serve with no condiments or add mayonnaise or mustard for an extra kick.

Reuben Rolls

⅓	cup mayonnaise	1	cup shredded Swiss cheese
1	tablespoon Dijon mustard	1	cup sauerkraut, rinsed
½	teaspoon caraway seeds		drained and patted dry
1	cup cooked corned beef,	1	package refrigerated pizza
	finely chopped		crust dough

In medium bowl, combine mayonnaise, mustard and caraway seeds. Add corned beef, cheese and sauerkraut, toss to blend well. Unroll dough onto large ungreased cookie sheet. Gently stretch to 14 x 12 inch rectangle. Cut dough lengthwise in half. Spoon half of filling on to each piece, spreading to within 1 inch of edges. From long side roll each jelly roll style; pinch to seal edges. Arrange rolls, seam-side down 3 inches apart. Bake in 425 degree oven for 10 minutes or until golden brown. Let stand 5 minutes and cut into 1 inch slices.

Sloppy Joe's

2	pounds ground beef	2	tablespoons vinegar
1	small bottle ketchup	1	tablespoon lemon juice
2	tablespoons sugar	¼	cup butter
1	cup chopped celery		Hamburger buns
1	tablespoon Worcestershire sauce		

In a large saucepan, cook all ingredients over medium-high heat until onion and celery are easily cut. Serve on buns. Makes 6 to 8 servings.

Chicken Barbecue

4	pounds chicken thighs	½	teaspoon granulated garlic
1	(18 ounce) container hickory smoked barbecue sauce	½	teaspoon minced onion
½	cup lemon juice		Sesame seed buns

Boil chicken thighs until tender. Shred chicken with fork. Heat remaining ingredients slowly to meld flavors. Mix sauce with meat and serve on sesame seed buns.

Dainty Ham and Cheese Sandwiches

SANDWICH

1½	pounds ham, chopped	1	cup shredded Swiss cheese
1	cup shredded Cheddar cheese	4	packages dainty dinner rolls

TOPPING

2	sticks margarine, melted	1	tablespoon Worcestershire sauce
3	tablespoons mustard	¾	cup chopped onion
1½	tablespoons poppy seeds		

Mix all the ham and cheese and set aside. Slice dinner rolls and lay them open. Divide ham and cheese mixture evenly between rolls and put top of rolls back on.

Prepare topping by mixing margarine, mustard, poppy seeds, Worcestershire sauce and onion. Stir until well mixed. Spread evenly on top of rolls. Bake at 350 degrees for 20 minutes.

Muffuletta

²/₃	cup olive oil	1	teaspoon minced garlic
½	cup chopped pimento stuffed green olives	1	(20 ounce) round Italian bread loaf
½	cup chopped black olives	¼	pound sliced salami
¼	cup chopped parsley (fresh or dried)	¼	pound sliced ham
1	teaspoon dried oregano	¼	pound sliced pepperoni
½	teaspoon pepper	¼	pound sliced mozzarella cheese
2	teaspoons lemon juice		

Combine first 8 ingredients, stirring well. Cover and chill. Cut bread loaf in half horizontally and scoop out a portion of the bottom to make a well for the olive mixture. Drain olive mixture and spoon half of mixture into bread shell. Top with layers of salami, ham, pepperoni and cheese. Spoon remaining olive mixture on top. Place top of bread on. Wrap in aluminum foil and bake at 325 degrees for 20 to 25 minutes. Cut to serve. Makes 8 servings.

If you'd prefer to roast peppers yourself, cut peppers into halves and remove seeds and membranes. Place cut side down on a foil-lined baking sheet. Bake at 425 degrees for 20 to 25 minutes or until skin in blackened. Place peppers in a paper bag and seal. Let stand for 10 to 30 minutes or until cool. Peel and slice. It's that easy!

Tailgate Baguettes

4	ounces cream cheese with chives and onions, softened	4	ounces sliced smoked turkey
1	tablespoon lemon juice	4	ounces sliced Virginia ham
1	tablespoon Dijon mustard	4	slices provolone or Swiss cheese
1/4	teaspoon garlic pepper	1	cup spinach leaves
1	(8 ounce) loaf sourdough bread or French bread	1	(7 ounce) jar roasted peppers, drained and sliced

Combine cream cheese, lemon juice, mustard and garlic pepper in a bowl and mix well. Cut bread lengthwise horizontally. Spread cut sides with cream cheese mixture. Layer turkey, cheese, peppers and spinach on bottom half of bread. Cover with top half and slice crosswise. Wrap in plastic wrap and chill for up to 6 hours. Serves 8.

Substitute the same amount of diced pimentos for the roasted peppers. Mix them with the cream cheese and it will do in a pinch!

Sides

INTELLIGENCE

A WOMAN'S PLACE IS IN THE CLASSROOM

Women in LaGrange in the nineteenth century held a distinct advantage over their counterparts in many other areas of the nation. They were fortunate enough to live in a community that placed great value on educating the more "delicate" sex. In the early part of the century, it was not even legal to bestow a degree on a woman. But that did not stop forward-thinking educators in Troup County from ringing the school bells for the female students who came from all over to take advantage of higher learning made available here.

Before the Civil War, LaGrange had already opened three female colleges: LaGrange Female Academy (later to become LaGrange College), Brownwood Institute and LaGrange Female Seminary (later to become Southern Female College). Not only was this significant for education in general – when LaGrange Female Academy was chartered in 1831, the only other college in the state was Franklin College (now operating as the University of Georgia) – but it was also a testament to the importance this community placed on the education of women.

Also remarkable is the fact that, just after the war, LaGrange College (called LaGrange Female College at the time) almost closed its doors for good when the trustees decided to sell the institution but found no buyers. Four local women staved off this fate by stepping up to run the college and proving to the board that the college was still viable. The many women and men (the college became permanently co-ed in 1953) who have earned degrees from LaGrange College since have the fabulous four of Mary Montgomery, Mary Evans Curtright, Florida Ferrell Presley and Avarilla Pryor to thank.

In more recent days, another woman led the charge for providing excellence in education to all. Ethel W. Kight, educated at Savannah State and Atlanta University, came to LaGrange in the 1940s as a sort of superintendent overseeing 34 small schools for black students. Together with the school board, she worked to consolidate the schools into fewer, greatly improved schools, one of which was named in her honor.

At the same time, Ethel worked against great obstacles to establish a library in LaGrange to serve the black population. Her initial efforts in a rented building with borrowed books captured the attention of the Callaway Foundation, which provided the funds for a new building. This library now bears her name. From the early days of LaGrange, phenomenal women have made sure that education is a primary ingredient in the lives of all. Strong women would not be complete without strong minds.

Sides

Cheese Apples

1	stick butter	1	cup sugar
¾	cup flour	1	(20 ounce) can sliced apples
½	pound Velveeta cheese, grated		

Cream butter and flour until blended. Add Velveeta and sugar to the blended butter and flour, mix well. Grease baking dish with butter just to cover the bottom of the dish. Place apples, undrained, into the dish. Spread the cheese mixture over the apples. Bake at 350 degrees for 30 to 40 minutes.

Asparagus with Tomato Confetti

1	pound peeled asparagus	½	cup olive oil
2	tomatoes	1	cup grated Parmesan cheese, divided
¼	cup chopped black olives		
2	scallions, chopped (including green stems)	¼	cup lightly toasted pine nuts or almonds
¼	cup balsamic vinegar		

In a sauté pan, place asparagus in a single layer. Cover with water. Cover pan and cook until tender (do not over cook). Drain and rinse in cold water. Place on a platter with tips at edge of plate. Cut tomatoes in half and squeeze gently to extract seeds and juice. Chop. Toss tomatoes, olives and scallions. Mix vinegar and olive oil, add ¼ cup Parmesan cheese and toss with tomato mixture. Spoon tomato mixture in lines over asparagus and drizzle the remaining dressing over entire dish. Sprinkle with pine nuts and remaining cheese. Cover and refrigerate for at least 1 hour.

Asparagus Straws

1	bundle thick asparagus spears (roughly 24 to 30)	1	teaspoon assorted crushed herbs
6-7	sheets phyllo dough, thawed and covered	12-14	slices prosciutto ham, cut crosswise
4	tablespoons unsalted butter, melted	4	ounces fine shredded Parmesan cheese
½	(8 ounce) package cream cheese		

Cook asparagus in steamer basket with over 1 inch of water, covered and for about 2 minutes until bright green. Drain and cool.

Preheat oven to 400 degrees. Place 1 sheet of phyllo dough at a time on work surface and brush with melted butter. Cut into 5 x 7 inch pieces. Whip cream cheese with herbs and spoon into a bag, cutting the tip off so as to pipe mixture. Place a slice of ham onto a piece of phyllo dough and pipe cream cheese along edge of ham. Arrange an asparagus spear along the same edge with tip showing above dough. Roll up. Repeat with remaining spears. Arrange wrapped spears on baking sheet lined with parchment paper and sprinkle cheese on top. Cover tips of the spears with foil to protect from burning. Bake for 6 to 9 minutes until golden brown. Serve warm.

Anise Morrison, Chef/Owner Ou lá lá

Using thicker, fresher asparagus spears is best, as thin asparagus will overcook in the oven. These can also be kept ready to bake in the refrigerator for up to half a day.

Chilled Asparagus with Pecans

2	tablespoons vegetable oil	⅛	cup soy sauce
1½	pounds fresh asparagus	¼	cup sugar
¾	cup finely chopped pecans		Black pepper sprinkled on
¼	cup cider vinegar		top

Cook asparagus in boiling water 6 to 7 minutes until tender but still bright green. Drain and rinse under cold water. Drain again. Arrange 1 or 2 layers in serving dish. Mix remaining ingredients and pour over asparagus, lifting so mixture penetrates to the bottom. Sprinkle liberally with pepper. Serve chilled. Serves 6.

May be marinated for up to 36 hours ahead and tastes better with at least 1 night of marinating.

Grilled Asparagus Rafts

16	thick asparagus spears	2	teaspoons sesame seeds, toasted
1	tablespoon low-sodium soy sauce	¼	teaspoon black pepper
1	teaspoon dark sesame oil		Salt
1	garlic clove, minced		

Prepare grill to high heat. Snap off tough ends of asparagus. Arrange 4 spears on a flat surface. Thread 2 (3 inch) skewers horizontally through spears 1 inch from end to form a raft. Repeat with remaining spears. Combine soy sauce, oil and garlic; brush evenly over asparagus rafts. Grill 3 minutes on each side or until crisp-tender. Sprinkle evenly with sesame seeds, pepper and salt.

Avocado Chutney

1	large ripe avocado		Juice of 1 lime
1	cup kernel corn	2	teaspoons ground cumin
1	small onion, finely chopped	1	teaspoon chili powder
1	red bell pepper, finely chopped	2	tablespoons chopped oregano
¼	cup olive oil	1	tablespoon chopped cilantro
2	tablespoons red wine vinegar		Salt and pepper to taste
4	cloves garlic, minced		

Peel and pit avocado, then mash the avocado in a large bowl. Add the corn, onion, bell pepper, olive oil, vinegar, garlic, lime juice and seasonings. Mix well. Cover and chill at least 5 hours.

Easy Pesto

1	cup chopped basil leaves	½	cup Parmesan cheese
3	cloves garlic	½	cup olive oil
½	cup pine nuts or walnuts		

In a blender, combine first 4 ingredients. Slowly add oil while blender is running. Makes approximately 1½ cups.

Use this easy recipe for your main chicken dishes, in any noodle dish, on sandwiches or for an easy bruschetta appetizer.

Hearty Baked Beans

1 (15 ounce) can kidney beans
1 (16 ounce) can pork and beans
1 pound ground chuck, browned and drained
1 bell pepper, chopped
1 medium onion, chopped

1 tablespoon chili powder
1 tablespoon Worcestershire sauce
½ teaspoon Tabasco sauce
1 cup ketchup
1 tablespoon yellow mustard

Combine all ingredients and pour into greased casserole. Bake at 400 degrees, stirring occasionally, for 30 to 40 minutes when beans thicken.

Caribbean Black Beans

3 strips bacon
½ cup onion, diced
½ cup red bell pepper
2 tablespoons garlic, minced

1 (30 ounce) can black beans, rinsed and drained
½ cup chicken broth
1 (15 ounce) can diced tomatoes

Sauté bacon in large pan over medium heat for 5 minutes. Remove from pan. Add onion and pepper. Sauté for 3 minutes. Stir in garlic, sauté for 1 minute. Strain bacon, beans, tomato and broth. Bring to boil. Reduce and simmer for 20 minutes. Season with salt and pepper. Makes 4 servings.

This dish goes wonderfully with pork tenderloin.

Bacon Wrapped Green Beans

1	package regular cut bacon	3	cans whole green beans

Preheat oven to 400 degrees. After opening the package of bacon, cut in half down the middle. Drain and empty the cans of green beans in a bowl. Take about 4 to 8 whole green beans depending on the size of bundle you desire and wrap them in a half a piece of bacon. If the beans are thin use 8, if the beans are thick use 4. You want a bundle to be a two bite portion and no more.

After wrapping a green bean bundle, place it seam down in an 8½ x 11 inch Pyrex dish. After the dish if full, cook until bacon is done. Cover with foil and cook for 30 minutes and then remove foil and continue to cook. Remove from oven once the bacon is cooked; it will not be crispy.

The great thing about this recipe is that it can also be prepared and/or cooked in advance and it reheats in the oven or microwave well.

Easy Green Beans

1	pound green beans	2-3 teaspoons Nature's
2	tablespoons garlic salt	Seasoning or salt and
3-4	tablespoons butter	pepper

Cut ends off green beans and wash well. Place ½ inch water in large pot with garlic salt and bring to a boil. Steam green beans for 10 minutes or until fork tender. In sauté pan, melt butter and Nature's Seasoning. Place green beans in butter for 2 to 3 minutes and eat.

Sweet and Sour Green Beans

2	(14½ ounce) cans French style green beans	1	small jar pimento
2	tablespoons oil	6	tablespoons sugar
½	small onion, chopped	6	tablespoons white vinegar

Sauté onion in oil until soft. Add 1 can of beans, drained, and 1 can of beans with liquid. Add pimento, sugar and vinegar. Heat on stove top.

This dish is best made ahead and reheated so that the beans soak up the flavor of the cooking liquid.

Walnut Broccoli

3	(10½ ounce) packages frozen, chopped broccoli	2	cups milk
½	cup butter	⅔	cup water
¼	cup all-purpose flour	6	tablespoons butter
2	teaspoons instant chicken bouillon	⅔	of a 7 ounce bag fine bread stuffing mix
		⅔	cup chopped walnuts

Cook broccoli until just tender; drain and place in shallow greased 9 x 13 inch baking dish. Melt ½ cup butter. Blend in flour and instant chicken bouillon; simmer, stirring for 3 to 4 minutes. Blend in milk and cook, stirring until thickened. Pour over broccoli. Heat water and butter together and pour over stuffing. Stir in nuts. Top broccoli with this mixture and bake in a preheated 400 degree oven for 20 minutes or until thoroughly heated through and stuffing begins to brown.

Broccoli and Cauliflower Parmesan

1 bunch broccoli	1 can cream of chicken soup
1 head cauliflower	Fresh grated Parmesan
1 stick of butter, melted	cheese
1 (8 ounce) carton sour cream	

Boil both broccoli and cauliflower until tender, but do not overcook. Mix melted butter, sour cream and soup together. Place broccoli and cauliflower in oblong baking dish. Pour soup mixture over vegetables. Grate fresh Parmesan cheese over the top. Bake at 350 degrees for 10 minutes.

Central Market Cauliflower Purée

1 pound cauliflower florets, chopped (about 5 cups)	4 tablespoons heavy cream
3 garlic cloves, minced	2 teaspoons butter
$2/3$ cup chicken broth	$1/4$ cup fresh grated Parmesan cheese
1 teaspoon salt	Fresh chives for garnish

Simmer cauliflower, garlic, broth and salt in a small, covered saucepan. Cook until cauliflower is very tender, about 10 minutes. Purée the mixture with cream, butter and Parmesan cheese in a food processor until smooth. Garnish with chives and serve immediately. Makes approximately 5 servings.

Copper Carrots

5	cups sliced carrots	¾	cup white vinegar
1	white onion	1	(10 ounce) can condensed tomato soup
1	green bell pepper		
½	cup vegetable oil	1	teaspoon mustard
1	teaspoon salt	1	teaspoon Worcestershire sauce
1	teaspoon pepper		
1	cup sugar		

Boil carrots until tender, then drain and cool. Slice onion and bell pepper thinly. Mix all other ingredients together. Layer carrots, onions, and bell pepper together in a large serving bowl. Pour all other ingredients over carrots. Cover and marinate for at least 12 hours.

Corn Pudding

1	tablespoon sugar	2	eggs, beaten
¼	cup butter	1	box Jiffy corn muffin mix
1	can creamed corn	1	(8 ounce) carton sour cream
1	can whole corn, drained		

Melt butter in a 2 quart casserole dish. Add sugar. Combine remaining ingredients and pour into casserole dish. Bake at 350 degrees for approximately 1 hour or until brown around edges and firm in the center. Serves 8.

Roasted Corn with Cumin and Lime

1	tablespoon fresh lime juice	2	teaspoons extra virgin olive oil
1	teaspoon ground cumin		
½	teaspoon salt	6	ears fresh corn, in the husk
¼	teaspoon freshly ground black pepper	2	limes, cut lengthwise into wedges

Heat grill or preheat oven to 500 degrees. In small bowl, whisk together lime juice, cumin, salt, pepper and oil. Prepare corn, one ear at a time. Pull off and discard 2 or 3 tough outer leaves. Carefully pull back remaining leaves, one at a time. Expose as much of the ear as possible without tearing husks completely off. Pull off and discard all the silk. Brush kernels with oil mixture, using just enough to coat lightly. Smooth folded leaves back into place, one by one, until ear is completely covered. Arrange corn on grill or place in oven. Roast 15 minutes. Turn ears 2 or 3 times on grill only. Serve corn immediately, accompanied by additional salt and lime wedges to squeeze over corn as it's eaten.

Kerri Vice, Owner/Chef Table Toppers Catering Co.

Steamed Honey Pears

4	pears	¼	cup honey
½	cup chopped dates	1	teaspoon finely grated orange peel
½	cup chopped figs		

Peel and core pears, set aside. Combine dates, figs and honey, orange peel in a bowl. Pack mixture into the cored pears. In a steamer, bring water to a boil. Place the stuffed pears in individual bowls or on a steaming tray. Steam the pears for about 30 minutes, checking frequently to avoid overcooking (pears should hold their shape). Remove the tray from the steamer and allow the pears to cool for about 30 minutes. Serve at room temperature.

Cheesy Mashed Potatoes

6	large potatoes, peeled and quartered	1/3	cup chopped onion
1	(8 ounce) package cream cheese	1	egg
1	cup shredded Cheddar cheese	2	teaspoons salt
1/2	cup sour cream	1/2	teaspoon pepper
			Shredded Cheddar, optional
			Parsley, optional

Place potatoes in a large saucepan; cover with water. Cover and bring to a boil. Cook for 20 to 25 minutes or until very tender; drain well.

In a mixing bowl, mash potatoes. Add cream cheese, Cheddar cheese, sour cream, onion, egg, salt and pepper; beat until fluffy. Transfer to a greased 2 quart baking dish. Cover and bake at 350 degrees for 40 to 45 minutes. Sprinkle with additional shredded Cheddar and parsley, if desired. Serves 10.

Roasted Potatoes

1/4	cup butter	1	teaspoon garlic salt
1	teaspoon dried Italian seasoning	2	pounds red potatoes, cubed

Preheat oven to 425 degrees. Melt butter in an 8 or 9 inch pan, then add seasoning and stir. Add potatoes and stir to coat. Bake for 45 minutes, stirring occasionally.

"Hoop" Potatoes

5 large red potatoes scrubbed, but not peeled, cut into 8 long ways
2 large white onions, chopped (frozen chopped onion works great)
4 ribs of celery, chopped

1 teaspoon salt
½ teaspoon pepper
½ teaspoon accent
1½ sticks butter
2 tablespoons parsley flakes
1 teaspoon paprika

Place potatoes in a greased 2 quart rectangle baking dish. Place the slices neatly in the dish, one overlapping the other. Put all of the ingredients on the potatoes. Slice thinly the butter, placing it evenly over the top of all the potatoes. Leave the paprika for last. Cover and bake at 350 degrees for approximately 45 plus minutes, basting several times. Remove cover and test until fork tender. Once tender, bake at 15 minutes without cover. Add more butter at any time, if needed. These can be put together and baked in advance. This dish reheats well in oven or microwave.

Sweet Potato and Apple Casserole

2 cups sweet potatoes, peeled and sliced
2 cups tart cooking apples, sliced

½ teaspoon salt
1 cup brown sugar
   Orange slices

Cook sweet potatoes in boiling, salted water for 15 minutes. In buttered casserole dish, alternately arrange slices of potato and apple. Sprinkle with salt and sugar. Top with orange slices to cover and bake at 350 degrees for 40 minutes or until apples are tender.

Mini Florentine Cups

1	(10 ounce) package frozen, chopped spinach, thawed and well drained	1	tablespoon grated Parmesan cheese
½	cup shredded mozzarella cheese	1	tablespoon finely chopped onion
⅓	cup light cream cheese spread	¼	teaspoon garlic powder
		24	slices deli style shaved oven roasted turkey breast

Preheat oven to 350 degrees. Mix all ingredients except turkey until well blended. Flatten turkey slices and place 1 slice in each of 24 miniature muffin pan cups. Fill each with 1½ teaspoons of spinach mixture. Bake for 15 minutes or until heated through. Serve warm. Makes 24 cups.

Spinach Artichoke Casserole

2	packages frozen chopped spinach, thawed	1	can water chestnuts, drained Tabasco sauce and Worcestershire sauce to taste
1	(3 ounce) package cream cheese		
1	stick butter	¼	cup grated or shredded fresh Parmesan cheese
1	can artichokes, drained		

Cook spinach, drain and chop. Put in butter and cream cheese, sliced water chestnuts, and sliced artichoke hearts. Season with Worcestershire sauce, Tabasco sauce. Sprinkle Parmesan cheese on top. Put in casserole dish, cover, and heat at 350 degrees until cheese melts, and it is warm throughout.

Squash Casserole

1	pound frozen yellow squash	½	stick butter
1	teaspoon sugar		Salt
1	egg		Pepper
½	cup mayonnaise		Ritz cracker crumbs
½	cup grated cheese		

Cook squash until tender and drain. Add butter and mash the two ingredients together. Mix sugar, egg, mayonnaise, cheese, salt and pepper. Pour mixture into a casserole dish and cover with cracker crumbs. Dot with melted butter. Bake at 350 for 35 to 40 minutes.

Broiled Tomatoes

4	large firm tomatoes	½	cup grated Parmesan cheese
	Spicy brown mustard	½	cup Italian-seasoned bread
½	teaspoon salt		crumbs
¼	teaspoon black pepper	¼	cup plus 2 tablespoons
⅛	teaspoon ground red pepper		butter, melted

Cut tomatoes in half crosswise. Pat cut surfaces of tomatoes with paper towel to remove excess moisture. Spread mustard over cut side of each tomato half. Combine salt and peppers in a small bowl; stir well. Sprinkle pepper mixture over top of each tomato half. Combine cheese, bread crumbs, and butter; stir well. Spoon breadcrumb mixture evenly over top of each tomato half. Place tomatoes in shallow baking dish. Bake at 350 degrees for 5 to 6 minutes. Broil 4 inches from heat 30 seconds or until lightly browned.

Sweet Acorn Squash

2	large acorn squash for method 1	½	cup light corn syrup
4	small acorn squash for method 2	½	cup melted butter
⅔	cup orange juice	1	tablespoon grated lemon peel
1	cup firmly packed light brown sugar	¼	teaspoon salt
			Olive oil (method 2 only)

Method 1: Only use large squash. Trim end from squash, cut into crosswise slices ¼ inch thick. Place slices in large lightly buttered shallow baking pan. Add orange juice. Cover with foil and bake at 350 degrees for 30 minutes. Combine brown sugar, corn syrup, butter, lemon peel and salt; pour over squash rings. Bake, uncovered, for 15 to 20 minutes longer. Baste occasionally, until squash is done and nicely glazed. Serves 8 to 10.

Method 2: Only use small squash. Cut acorn squash in half from end to end. Seed the squash and brush with olive oil. Cut thin slice off the skin side of each half, to stabilize the half when baked the second time. Place skin side up on a baking sheet. Bake at 350 degrees for 30 to 40 minutes. Remove from oven and scoop out tender meat of squash, being careful not to get too much as to destroy the skin. Mix the meat with remaining ingredients and return to skins. Place back in oven for 15 to 20 minutes until starts to caramelize. Serves 8.

This is a favorite for autumn and makes a gorgeous presentation.

Garden Fresh Tomato Pie

1	pre-cooked pie crust (deep dish if frozen)	1	cup mayonnaise
4	ripe tomatoes	1	cup grated Chedder cheese
10	fresh basil leaves	1	cup grated mozzarella cheese
3	green onions		Salt

Peel and slice the tomatoes. Place the tomatoes in a colander or on paper towels. Sprinkle the tomatoes with salt on each side and let drain for about 10 minutes. Dice the green onions and fresh basil. Place tomatoes in pie crust layering the onions and basil.

Mix together the mayonnaise and two cheeses and cover the top of the pie. Bake at 350 degrees for about 30 minutes.

Marinated Tomatoes

¼	cup oil	2	teaspoons prepared mustard
1	clove garlic, crushed	1	teaspoon salt
1	tablespoon sugar	2-3	large tomatoes, peeled and quartered
¼	teaspoon pepper		
2	tablespoons cider vinegar		

Mix all ingredients, adding tomatoes last. Stir, cover and refrigerate for several hours before serving. Makes 4 servings.

Zucchini Casserole

4-5 zucchini	Parsley, to taste
1 egg	Salt and pepper, to taste
1 cup whipping cream	1 cup grated Gruyère cheese
1 clove garlic (minced)	

Clean zucchini and cut into slices. Steam zucchini and allow to remain a little firm. In a bowl; mix together egg, whipping cream, garlic, parsley, salt and pepper. Spread zucchini into casserole dish and pour mixture over top. Cover with cheese and bake at 450 degrees for 35 minutes.

Hawaiian Bread Holiday Stuffing

2 loaves Hawaiian bread or egg bread	1 tablespoon fresh thyme leaves
1 cup pineapple chunks, drained	1 pound link sausage, cut in ¼ inch slices
1 cup cranberries (any type)	1 tablespoon oil
1 cup chestnuts, chopped and drained	2 medium onions, chopped
1 tablespoon fresh sage, chopped	5 stalks celery, chopped
	5 cloves minced garlic
	1 cup whole milk
	1 cup chicken broth

Tear or slice bread into bite-size pieces. Spread out on sheet pan. Bake just until toasted and dry. Place in a large bowl. Mix pineapple, cranberries, chestnuts, sage and thyme in bread bowl and set aside. Brown sausage in pan with oil. Drain excess oil and add onion and celery. Sweat 10 minutes. Add garlic and cook 3 minutes. Add mixture to bread bowl. Add milk and broth. Stir to mix thoroughly. Pour into casserole dish. Bake at 350 degrees for 30 to 40 minutes.

Grits and Cheese Stuffed Shells

1	cup cooked grits	1	teaspoon garlic powder
1	cup ricotta cheese	1	(12 ounce) package gumbo shells, cooked and drained
1½	cups grated Parmesan cheese	1	(1 pound, 10 ounce) jar spaghetti sauce
1	egg	1	cup mozzarella cheese
2	teaspoons salt		
½	teaspoon black pepper		

Combine grits, ricotta cheese, ½ cup Parmesan cheese, egg, salt, pepper and garlic powder in a bowl. Stuff shells with grits and cheese mixture. Cover bottom of 9 x 13 inch casserole dish with ½ jar spaghetti sauce. Arrange stuffed shells in dish, open sides down, and pour remaining sauce over shells. Cover and bake at 350 for 20 minutes. Uncover, sprinkle with mozzarella cheese and remaining Parmesan cheese. Bake additional 8 to 10 minutes or until cheese bubbles.

Add 1 cup chopped, cooked and drained spinach to filling.

Macaroni and Cheese

1 (8 ounce) package elbow macaroni
1 (10¾ ounce) can cream of celery soup, undiluted

1 small grated onion
4 cups shredded Cheddar cheese
1½ cups mayonnaise

Cook macaroni according to package directions. Drain. Combine macaroni, soup, onion and 3½ cups of Cheddar cheese. Pour into a greased 12 x 8 x 2 inch baking dish. Sprinkle remaining Cheddar cheese over top. Bake at 350 degrees for 30 minutes. Makes 6 to 8 servings.

Penne with Spicy Vodka Tomato Cream Sauce

¼ teaspoon extra virgin olive oil
4 cloves garlic, minced
½ teaspoon crushed red pepper flakes
1 (28 ounce) can crushed tomatoes
¾ teaspoon salt
½ pound penne pasta cooked and drained

¼ cup vodka
½ cup heavy whipping cream
¼ cup chopped fresh parsley,
1 pound boiled shrimp, peeled and deveined
½ cup grated Parmesan cheese
1 (8 ounce) package fresh mushrooms

In large skillet, heat oil over medium heat. Add garlic, red pepper and mushrooms, stirring until garlic is golden brown. Add shrimp, tomatoes and salt and bring to boil. Reduce heat and simmer 15 minutes. Add vodka and cream and bring to a boil. Reduce heat to low. Stir in pasta and mix. Add fresh parsley and Parmesan cheese and serve.

Consommé Rice

2   cans consommé soup,   ⅓   cup chopped onion
     undiluted   4-5 tablespoons butter
1   cup regular white converted
     rice

Sauté chopped onion and rice in butter until lightly browned. Pour rice mixture and undiluted soups into a buttered 1½ quart casserole dish. Mix and cover. Bake at 350 degrees for 1 hour or until all the liquid is absorbed. Fluff with a fork and serve.

Curry Chicken and Rice

6   cups cooked rice   ⅔   cup minced green onion tops
5-6 cups cooked diced chicken   ½   cup chopped fresh parsley
1½ cups toasted pecans

Combine above and toss well. Add dressing and toss. Chill thoroughly.

DRESSING
1½ cups mayonnaise   2   tablespoons curry powder
4   tablespoons soy sauce   2   tablespoons garlic vinegar

Combine ingredients in saucepan and heat thoroughly.

Mexican Rice

1	cup instant rice	½	cup shredded Monterey Jack cheese
2	cups water		
1	(8 ounce) carton sour cream	1	can Rotel tomatoes, drained
1	cup shredded sharp Cheddar cheese	½	cup butter

Mix rice and water and cook in microwave until rice is done. Let cool. Mix rice with sour cream. Spread half mixture into a 1½ quart casserole dish. Top with cheeses and tomatoes. Spread other half of rice mixture on top. Chop butter into pieces and sprinkle on top. Bake at 350 degrees for 30 minutes.

French Rice

1	cup instant rice, uncooked	1	(4½ ounce) can sliced mushrooms
1	(10½ ounce) can French onion soup	1	(8 ounce) can sliced water chestnuts, optional
½	cup melted butter		

Combine soup and butter and stir well. Drain mushrooms and water chestnuts, reserving liquid. Add enough water to reserved liquid to equal 1½ cups. Add mushrooms, water chestnuts, liquid and rice to soup mixture. Stir well. Pour into lightly greased 10 x 6 x 2 inch baking dish. Bake at 350 for 1 hour.

Entrées

CREATIVITY

LAGRANGE WOMEN BRING MUSIC AND ART TO LIFE

"She had learned somewhere ... that there is an art in living, that life itself is the finest of the fine arts." That's what a college friend said of Lucy May Stanton, a famous artist who studied in LaGrange. This is something many local women in the late 1800s came to realize. While cities like New York, Boston and Paris were hotspots for the arts, LaGrange developed its own powerhouse for artistic talent. At the heart of this talent were LaGrange's female colleges. Lucy May Stanton studied art at LaGrange's Southern Female College and became one of Georgia's most highly acclaimed painters. Her works are represented in the permanent collections of the Metropolitan Museum of Art, the Museum of Fine Arts in Boston, the National Portrait Gallery, and the Philadelphia Museum of Art.

After the death of her mother, Lucy's father married Sallie Cox, who was a violinist and the daughter of Southern Female College's president. Sallie and her sister, Alice, studied music in Boston and New York and went on to become renowned musicians, as well as instructors at Southern Female College. Alice, who studied piano with a pupil of Franz Liszt, was praised in the Boston Music Journal and was quoted as being "the most promising pianist America ever produced."

Troup County voices were also heard throughout the country. LaGrange native Mary Virginia Dunson Evans studied at the Boston Conservatory and went on to become a nationally known singer. She was one of the first people in the world to make a voice recording. "Jennie" later returned to LaGrange, as an instructor at LaGrange Female College and a member of the College Concert Company, a traveling musical group that raised money for the college.

During this time, one of the most popular art forms was portraiture. Commissioned nationally for her portraits, Adah Mendenhall Awtrey not only graduated from Southern Female College, but also later served as head of the college's Art Department. Another popular artistic medium during the day was "theme painting." LaGrange native Maggie Evans, who was said to be "a genius in art," often taught her art classes by giving students a theme such as "sun setting on a brook" or "an evening in Pompeii." Art exhibits based on these themes were then on display for LaGrange residents to enjoy.

Women in the arts even played a role in the Civil War, during which a precursor to the USO was born in LaGrange. Under the direction of Mrs. Sherwood Swanson, LaGrange's Electa Club (named for the group's teenage star, Electa Forbes) wrote and acted out original plays that children often performed at the local Confederate hospital. The plays not only entertained the soldiers, but also raised money for the war. Whether it was music, painting or writing, LaGrange women brought beauty and joy to life through their works of art.

Entrées

Seasonings

Grilled Beef Tenderloin with Red Wine and Pistachios

Don't throw away left over wine. Freeze into ice cubes for future use in casseroles and sauces.

2   cups beef or veal stock
2   cups dry red wine
½   cup roasted garlic cloves
½   cup chopped shallots
½   cup chopped fresh parsley
1   dash salt
1   dash fresh ground pepper

¼   cup toasted pistachios-chopped
¼   cup toasted sunflower seeds-chopped
2   pounds beef tenderloin
2   tablespoons olive oil

Preheat grill or broiler. In a large saucepan-combine stock, red wine, 3 tablespoons of roasted garlic, shallots and ¼ cup of the parsley. Bring to simmer over medium heat and cook until reduced to coat the back of a spoon. (It says about 20 minutes, but it took us about an hour.) Transfer to a blender and purée until smooth. Strain through a fine sieve into another saucepan, then adjust the salt and pepper. Stir in remaining parsley, then reduce to a low heat. In a small bowl, combine the remaining garlic, the pistachios, sunflower seeds, and 2 tablespoons of the red wine sauce. Mix well. Rub the steaks with oil, grill to desired temperature. Brush the tops of the steaks with a small amount of red wine sauce, then press the steaks top side down into the pistachio mixture, coating them well. (We pretty much just completely covered the steaks with the nuts and then poured all the sauce over the top.)

Grilled Flank Steak

1 (1½ pound) flank steak	½ cup soy sauce
1 cup vegetable oil	¼ cup red wine
½ cup firmly packed brown sugar	1 tablespoon minced garlic
	1 teaspoon ground ginger

Trim excess fat from steak. Place steak in a shallow dish. Combine oil, and remaining ingredients, stirring well. Pour over steak. Cover dish and marinate in the refrigerator overnight, turning occasionally. Remove steak from marinade and reserve remaining marinade. Grill, covered, over medium coals for 6 to 8 minutes on each side, basting 2 or 3 times with reserved marinade. To serve, slice steak across the grain into thin slices.

Chuck Roast Barbecue

1 (2-3 pound) boneless chuck roast, trimmed	1 teaspoon beef bouillon granules
2 large onions, finely chopped	½ teaspoon dry mustard
¾ cup cola beverage	½ teaspoon chili powder
¼ cup Worcestershire sauce	½ cup prepared BBQ sauce
1 tablespoon apple vinegar	2 teaspoons butter
2 cloves garlic, minced	

Combine roast and chopped onions in a slow cooker. Combine cola and next 7 ingredients (reserve ½ cup in refrigerator). Pour remaining mixture over roast and onion. Cook covered on high for 6 hours or on low for 10 hours or until roast is very tender. Drain and shred roast (keep cooked onions with roast). Keep warm while you prepare sauce. Combine reserved ½ cup cola mixture, BBQ sauce and butter in a small pan. Cook mixture over medium heat, stirring constantly until thoroughly heated. Pour over shredded roast and onions.

Dutch Oven Pot Roast with Gravy

1	(2-3 pound) bottom round or rump roast	2	tablespoons canola oil
6-8	garlic cloves	1½	cups water, divided, plus extra
	Coarse salt	3	tablespoons flour
	Fresh ground black pepper		

Trim fat from roast. Using a small, sharp knife, make 6 to 8 holes throughout the roast by inserting the knife 2 inches into the roast and twisting it. Fill each hole with a peeled garlic clove, making sure the clove is pressed into the meat until it's not visible. Sprinkle with salt and pepper. Heat oil in Dutch oven over medium-high. Brown the roast on all sides. Reduce heat to low and add 1 cup of water. Cover and cook for 6 hours. Add extra water if needed, keeping the water level 1 inch deep. Do not let boil. Ladle juices over the roast several times throughout cooking. After several hours of cooking, slice the roast about halfway through, making sure you don't cut completely through the meat. When roast is done, place on a platter and slice through. Remove garlic cloves if desired.

To make gravy, whisk flour into ½ cup cold water, then pour into a pan. Increase heat to medium and whisk occasionally while bringing mixture to a low boil. Reduce heat to simmer until gravy is thickened.

Sullin's Roast

3 pound London broil or top round beef roast	½ cup Wesson oil
Adolf's meat tenderizer	2 tablespoons soy sauce
¼ cup wine vinegar with garlic	1 clove garlic, crushed

Poke roast with fork about every 2 inches all over both sides. Sprinkle with meat tenderizer generously. Mix the rest of the ingredients and marinate roast overnight or for 3 to 4 hours at room temperature. Must be turned once. Sear meat on a grill 1 to 2 minutes per side. Cook 8 minutes on each side.

To make this recipe easier, used crushed garlic from a jar.

Cheesy Lasagna

2 pounds ground beef	1 teaspoon salt
1 onion, chopped	9 lasagna noodles
1 tablespoon parsley	12 slices American cheese
1 teaspoon garlic powder	1 (8 ounce) carton sour cream
1 teaspoon sugar	2-3 cups mozzarella cheese
2 (16 ounce) cans tomato sauce	

Brown ground beef and onion, drain. Add parsley, salt, garlic powder, sugared and tomato sauce. Simmer for 1 hour. Layer noodles on bottom of dish, cover with 4 slices of American cheese. Spread on sour cream and sprinkle with meat sauce and mozzarella. Repeat 2 more times. Bake at 350 degrees uncovered for 30 minutes.

Baked Spaghetti

1	(28 ounce) can diced tomatoes	½	teaspoon garlic powder
1	(16 ounce) can tomato sauce	½	teaspoon black pepper
1	cup water	2	bay leaves
2	cloves garlic, minced	12	ounces thin spaghetti or angel hair pasta
½	cup finely diced onion	1½	pounds lean ground beef
2	teaspoons sugar	1½	cups grated Cheddar cheese
1	teaspoon dried basil	1½	cups grated Monterey Jack cheese
1	teaspoon dried oregano		
1½	teaspoons coarse salt		

Combine first 12 ingredients in a large pot or Dutch oven and bring to a boil over high heat. Cover and reduce heat to low, simmer for 45 to 50 minutes. Brown ground beef in a large skillet until fully cooked with no pink color. Drain beef and carefully add to the tomato mixture. Continue cooking on low heat for 15 to 20 minutes more. At this point pre-heat oven to 350 degrees. While sauce is simmering, cook pasta according to package directions. Using a 13 x 9 x 2 inch baking dish, cover the bottom of dish with a layer of sauce, then add half of the pasta and 1 cup of the cheese. Add another layer of sauce, pasta then another cup of cheese, and add all remaining sauce on top. Bake for 25 minutes, the sprinkle remaining cheese over the top. Cook 5 minutes more, then remove from oven and let sit for 5 minutes before serving. May be prepared in 2 smaller dishes if desired.

Marvelous Meatballs

MEATBALLS

1½ pounds lean ground beef	⅔ cup milk
2 eggs, beaten	3 slices crumbled bread
1 cup grated carrots	1 small onion, chopped
1 cup grated cheese	

SAUCE

⅓ cup brown sugar	2 tablespoons mustard
1 cup ketchup	

Combine all meatball ingredients and form into 3 inch balls. Place in baking dish. Mix sauce ingredients together and pour over meatballs. Bake at 350 degrees for 1 hour. Serves 8.

Meatballs and Rice in Consommé

1 pound ground chuck	2 tablespoons chopped celery
1 teaspoon salt	and leaves
⅛ teaspoon black pepper	1 small onion, chopped
Olive oil	1 can condensed consommé
¼ cup chopped bell pepper	1 can water
	⅔ cup rice

Mix ground chuck, salt and black pepper. Form into small meatballs. Brown slowly on all sides in a skillet using a small amount olive oil. Add bell pepper, celery, and onions and cook 5 minutes longer. Add rice, consommé and water. Bring to boil, cover and simmer gently stirring occasionally for 20 minutes or until rice is tender and liquid is absorbed. Serves 4.

Betty Daniel, Owner and Chef, Taste of Lemon

If desired, 3 bouillon cubes dissolved in 3 cups of hot water may be substituted for consommé. Also, you could add a little red wine and a pinch of thyme.

Carolina Holiday Grilled Lamb

1	leg of lamb, deboned	3	teaspoons salt
1	cup olive oil	1/4	teaspoon black pepper
2/3	cup lemon juice	1½	teaspoons dried sage
3	minced garlic cloves	1½	teaspoons dried rosemary
2	bay leaves	1½	teaspoons dried thyme
6	sprigs of parsley		

Remove all fat from lamb. Cut entire leg of lamb into serving size(s) fillets and butterfly as the piece allows. Combine all ingredients except lamb in a bowl to form marinate. Place lamb fillets in a flat Pyrex dish and pour the marinade over meat. Turn to coat each piece of meat well. Marinate meat over night for 24 hours turning several times. Sear each side of lamb over hot coals of the grill (approximately 3 minutes). Remove meat and lower grill heat. Place meat back on the grill and continue to cook it brushing several times with marinate. Outside of meat should be crusty and inside should be pink when done.

Blackened Chicken Breasts

6	boneless, skinless chicken breasts	2	teaspoons paprika
6	tablespoons butter or margarine, melted	1½	teaspoons coarse salt
		1	teaspoon ground black pepper
1	teaspoon garlic powder	1/4	teaspoon white pepper
1	teaspoon onion powder	1/4	teaspoon cumin
1	teaspoon cayenne pepper	1	teaspoon dried thyme

Slice chicken breasts in half and pound to flatten. Brush each piece with butter. Combine all other ingredients and sprinkle both sides of chicken breasts. Cover and refrigerate for 30 minutes. Cook in a heavy skillet over high heat for 6 to 8 minutes per side. Serves 6.

If you're cooking for less than 6, just prepare mixture as stated, but store in an airtight container for the next time you want to prepare this dish. It will keep for several months.

Avalanche Chicken

CHICKEN

6-8 whole chicken breasts,
  boned and halved
3 tablespoons lemon juice
¼ teaspoon salt
¼ teaspoon black pepper
½ teaspoon celery salt
2 teaspoons paprika

2 cans cream of mushroom
  soup
1 can cream of celery soup
½ cup dry sherry or white wine
2 garlic cloves, minced
¼ cup Parmesan cheese

TOPPINGS

2 cups shredded Cheddar
  cheese
2 cups chopped celery
2 cups diced tomatoes
1 cup chopped green onion
2 cups slivered almonds
1 (16 ounce) can crushed
  pineapple

1 can sliced mushrooms
1 (6 ounce) can sliced water
  chestnuts
1 bag chow mien noodles
1 small bag coconut flakes

Rinse chicken breasts, pat dry. Season with lemon juice, salt, pepper, celery salt and paprika. Place in large crock pot. In medium bowl mix soups with sherry and garlic. Pour over chicken and sprinkle with Parmesan cheese. Cover and cook on low for 8 to 10 hours or on high for 4 to 5 hours. After done, cool chicken and pull meat off the bones and shred. Add meat back into crock pot. Serve toppings in individual dishes. Serves 10 to 12.

This dish is best served over rice and with a side salad so the same toppings can be used for it.

Brandicot Chicken

2	teaspoons cornstarch	1	clove minced garlic
¼	cup soy sauce	¼	teaspoon ground ginger
¼	cup apricot preserves	1	tablespoon brandy
2	tablespoons sugar		Pepper to taste
2	tablespoons white vinegar	4	chicken breasts

Stir together cornstarch and soy sauce. Stir in preserves, sugar, vinegar, garlic, ginger and pepper. Cook over medium-high heat until thick and bubbling. Remove from heat and stir in brandy. Place chicken in casserole and pour sauce over top. Bake 30 minutes at 375 degrees then turn pieces and bake until tender.

Cheesy Chicken Spaghetti

1	large chicken, cut up	1	(12 ounce) package vermicelli
4	tablespoons butter	1	(15 ounce) can Rotel
1	(15 ounce) can English peas		tomatoes
1	onion, chopped	1	(10¾ ounce) can cream of
1	bell pepper, chopped		mushroom soup
1	(4¼ ounce) can sliced	1	pound Velveeta cheese
	mushrooms		

Boil chicken in salted water for 20 to 30 minutes until tender. Remove chicken, de-bone and set aside. Cook vermicelli in broth for 10 minutes. Sauté onion and bell pepper in butter in small frying pan. Add soup and cheese to vermicelli until melted. Stir in onion, bell pepper, chicken, mushrooms Rotel and peas. Pour into large greased casserole dish. Bake at 350 degrees for 35 to 40 minutes. Serves 10 to 12.

Chicken Brunch Ring

1 cup mayonnaise
2 tablespoons Dijon mustard
2 tablespoons parsley
1 tablespoon finely chopped onion
1 (10 ounce) can chunk white chicken

4 slices bacon, crisply cooked and crumbled
1 cup Swiss cheese, divided
2 (8 ounce) packs refrigerated crescent rolls
2 plum tomatoes, thinly sliced
Bell pepper
Lettuce, shredded

Preheat oven to 350 degrees. Combine mayonnaise, mustard, parsley and onion. In another bowl, flake chicken and add bacon. Add ¾ cup of cheese and ⅓ cup of the mayonnaise mixture; mix well. Separate crescent triangles and place in a circle on a cookie sheet or round baking stone with wide ends overlapping in the center and points toward the outside. Scoop chicken mixture onto widest end of each triangle. Bring point of triangle up over filling and tuck under wide ends at center of ring. Filling will not be completely covered. Place a tomato slice on ring where triangles do not meet. Bake 20 to 25 minutes or until deep golden brown. Remove from oven and immediately sprinkle with remaining cheese. Cut top off bell pepper and scoop out insides. Fill with remaining mayonnaise mixture and place in center of ring. Arrange lettuce around pepper. Cut into servings.

Chicken and Wild Rice

1	medium onion, chopped	1	can French style green
1	tablespoon butter		beans, drained
3	cups cooked, diced chicken	1	cup mayonnaise
1	(6 ounce) package long grain	1	(8 ounce) can sliced water
	and wild rice, cooked		chestnuts, drained
1	can cream of celery soup		Salt and pepper
1	(4 ounce) jar pimentos		

Sauté onion in butter. Mix all ingredients. Pour into 3 quart casserole dish and bake at 350 degrees for 25 minutes.

Chicken Orange Roll-Ups

6	chicken breasts	½	cup butter cut into pieces
¼	cup melted butter	2	cups orange juice
1	tablespoon Triple Sec or	1	tablespoon tarragon
	orange extract	1	teaspoon salt
6	thin slices ham	1	teaspoon grated orange peel
	Flour	6	(½ inch) thick orange slices
2	eggs, lightly beaten		Parsley sprigs or fresh
	Seasoned bread crumbs		tarragon, optional for garnish

Remove and discard chicken bones. Flatten chicken with a meat mallet or rolling pin. Marinate chicken in a mixture of ¼ cup melted butter and Triple Sec for 10 to 15 minutes. Place 1 ham slice on each chicken piece and roll up as for jelly rolls. Secure with wooden toothpicks. Coat chicken rolls with flour. Dip chicken into beaten eggs, then roll in bread crumbs. Arrange chicken in a single layer in a 9 x 12 inch baking dish. Dot with butter. Bake at 400 degrees for 15 minutes.

Combine orange juice, tarragon, salt and orange peel in a bowl and mix well. Spoon over chicken. Reduce the oven temperature to 350 degrees. Bake for 35 minutes or until chicken is cooked through, basting occasionally.

To serve, place chicken over orange slices on individual serving plates. Spoon pan drippings over the top. Garnish with parsley sprigs.

Chicken Pot Pie

PIE

2	cups diced cooked chicken	1	can cream of celery soup
2	cans cream of chicken soup	1	(14 ounce) can chicken broth
1	(32 ounce) package frozen mixed vegetables		Salt and pepper to taste

CRUST

1	stick butter at room temperature	1	cup self-rising flour
		1	cup milk

Spread chicken in a greased 13 x 9 inch dish. Mix soups, broth and vegetables. Pour over chicken. To prepare crust, cut butter into flour with a fork until crumbly. Add milk and stir. It will look runny, but pour over casserole. Put a few pats of butter across top and bake at 350 degrees for 1 to 1½ hours or until crust is golden.

Cilantro Chicken

2	tablespoons olive oil		Juice of 1 lime
½	teaspoon chili powder	4	skinless, boneless chicken breasts halves
¼	teaspoon garlic powder		Salt and pepper
¼	teaspoon cilantro		

Mix olive oil, chili powder, garlic powder, cilantro and lime juice in a small bowl. Place chicken in a shallow dish; sprinkle with salt and pepper on both sides and drizzle with seasoned oil. Cover and marinate in refrigerator for 20 minutes. Place chicken on broiler pan coated with cooking spray and broil 6 minutes on each side or until done. Cut chicken in thin slices and plate.

This dish is great to serve atop Southwestern Black Bean Dip (see appetizers) with a dollop of sour cream.

Creamy Chicken Pasta

12	ounces angel hair pasta	2	cups sour cream
2	cups cooked diced chicken	1	teaspoon garlic salt
½	cup softened butter	1	tablespoon parsley flakes
2	cans cream of chicken soup		Parmesan cheese

Break pasta into fourths and cook according to package directions. Meanwhile, in a large bowl, combine remaining ingredients. Stir in cooked pasta, then pour into a greased baking dish. Sprinkle with Parmesan cheese and bake at 350 degrees for 45 to 60 minutes or until bubbly.

Italian Stuffed Chicken Breasts

4	thick boneless, skinless chicken breasts	¼	teaspoon garlic powder
½	teaspoon coarse salt	2	ounces fontina cheese
¼	teaspoon fresh ground pepper	¼	cup flour
1	teaspoon dried basil	1	cup fine, dry bread crumbs
1	teaspoon dried oregano	1	egg, lightly beaten
1	teaspoon dried thyme	1½	tablespoons butter
		⅓	cup dry, white wine

Preheat oven to 350 degrees. Spray a 2 quart baking dish with cooking spray and set aside. Cut a small pocket in the thick part of each chicken breast; sprinkle inside and outside with salt and pepper. Combine basil, oregano, thyme and garlic in small bowl. Remove and discard the rind from cheese and cut into small pieces. Toss the cheese with half of the herb mixture and insert into the pockets of each breast. Pour the flour and bread crumbs onto plates and the egg in a bowl. Dredge the chicken in the flour, egg and bread crumbs in that order. Place in baking dish. Combine butter in wine in small saucepan over low heat until butter melts. Stir in the remainder of the herb mixture and pour over chicken. Bake for 35 minutes of until chicken reaches internal temperature of 170 degrees. Spoon juices over chicken and cook under the broiler just until the top browns. Serve immediately. Serves 4.

King Ranch Chicken Casserole

1 large onion, chopped	1 (10 ounce) can Rotel
1 large green bell pepper, chopped	tomatoes and green chiles
2 tablespoons butter	1 teaspoon chili powder
2 cups chopped cooked chicken	¼ teaspoon salt
1 (10¾ ounce) can cream of chicken soup, undiluted	¼ teaspoon garlic powder
1 (10¾ ounce) can cream of mushroom soup, undiluted	¼ teaspoon pepper
	12 (6 inch) yellow corn tortillas
	2 cups shredded Cheddar cheese, divided

Sauté onion and bell pepper in butter in a large skillet over medium-high heat for 5 minutes or until tender. Stir in chicken and next 7 ingredients, remove from heat. Tear tortilla pieces in bottom of a lightly greased 13 x 9 inch baking dish. Top with one-third of chicken mixture and ⅔ cup cheese. Repeat layers twice. Bake for 35 minutes at 350 degrees.

Mama's Cornflake Chicken

½ stick butter	1 can cream of mushroom soup
1 can evaporated milk	½ soup can water, plus extra if needed
2 cups cornflake crumbs, processed until a bit coarse	Salt and pepper
4 chicken breasts	

Melt butter in ovenproof baking dish. Pour milk into separate bowl. Place Cornflakes into separate bowl. Dip the chicken into milk and then into cornflakes and place in baking dish.

Stir together the soup and water. Stir in left over milk and cornflakes and pour over chicken. Add salt and pepper to taste. Add water as needed to keep chicken from being dry. Bake at 350 degrees for 1 hour.

Anise Morrison, Chef/Owner Ou lá lá

One of this chefs all time favorites — served with biscuits, of course!

"Miss Jane's" Crescent Roll Chicken

3	cups cooked chicken	½	cup chopped onions
1	can cream of chicken soup	1	can crescent rolls
1	(8 ounce) can mushroom stems and pieces, drained	½	cup slivered almonds, optional
1	can Chinese water chestnuts, drained	⅔	cup shredded sharp Cheddar cheese
⅔	cup mayonnaise		Butter
½	cup chopped celery		

Cook first 7 ingredients in saucepan until hot and bubbly. Pour into 12 x 9 inch or 13 x 9 inch casserole dish. Separate crescent rolls and place over mixture. Combine slivered almonds and cheese and spread over top. Dot with butter. Bake for 20 to 25 minutes at 375 degrees or until golden brown.

Anise Morrison, Chef/Owner Ou lá lá

This dish does very well reheated.

Southern Hot Wings

WINGS

40-50 chicken wings   **Vegetable oil**

SAUCE

4 cups Crystal hot sauce   **½ teaspoon white pepper**
2 cups butter   **½ teaspoon red wine vinegar**
1 teaspoon cayenne pepper

Heat oil in deep fryer or skillet over medium-high heat until hot. Cook chicken wings until light medium brown. Drain. Mix all sauce ingredients in container with lid. Add wings and shake or stir. Leave lid on container to let wings steam in the sauce a few moments before serving.

If you're looking for a milder taste, just decrease the amount of cayenne pepper.

Tuscan Chicken with Tomato Basil Relish

3-4 boneless, skinless chicken   **¼ cup sliced, drained sweet**
**   breasts**   **   pimentos**
**   Salt and pepper**   **¼ cup fresh basil leaves**
½ cup diced plum tomatoes   **½ teaspoon balsamic vinegar**
2 tablespoons diced red onion

Flatten chicken breasts between plastic wrap to ½ inch thickness. Heat skillet on medium-high and spray with olive oil cooking spray. Season chicken with salt and pepper and cook 3 minutes per side. Remove from heat and set aside. Mix tomatoes, onion, pimentos, basil and vinegar. Serve relish over chicken breasts.

Island Pork Tenderloin with Mojo Salsa

PORK RUB

1	tablespoon paprika	½	teaspoon salt
1	tablespoon chili powder	2	pounds pork tenderloin
1	tablespoon dried oregano		

MOJO BASTING SAUCE

¾	cup orange juice	1	habanero pepper, seeded and minced
2	tablespoons lime juice		
1	tablespoon minced garlic	1	tablespoon honey
1	teaspoon salt	1	tablespoon olive oil

MOJO SALSA

2	cups diced mango	¼	cup mojo sauce before adding honey and oil
1	tablespoon chopped cilantro		

Mix all ingredients of rub together and rub tenderloins with it. Pace on prepared pan. Combine mojo sauce ingredients except for honey and oil. Reserve ¼ cup for salsa. Whisk in honey and oil. Broil meat 3 minutes and baste with sauce. Broil 5 more minutes, flip and baste again. Broil additional 12 to 15 minutes. Meat should reach 145 degrees internal temperature. Continue basting through this process. Remove meat and tent with foil. Let stand 5 minutes. Slice and serve with mojo salsa.

Italian Baked Pork Chops

4	pork chops, thick cut	2	cloves garlic
1	large onion	1	(16 ounce) can stewed tomatoes
1	large bottle light Caesar dressing		

Combine all ingredients in a baking dish cover with foil and bake at 350 degrees for 1 to 1½ hours or until pork chops are tender.

Marinated Pork Tenderloin

1	package of 2 pork tenderloins, trimmed	2	tablespoons brown sugar
1/4	cup soy sauce	1/4	cup canola oil
4	cloves garlic, peeled and sliced	1	teaspoon coarse salt
		1/4	teaspoon ground ginger

Trim fat from tenderloins and place in a gallon-size zip-top plastic bag. Add all ingredients to bag, seal and turn to coat. Marinate in refrigerator for at least 8 to 10 hours or overnight. Remove tenderloins and discard marinade. Grill over medium heat for 20 to 30 minutes or until meat thermometer registers 160 degrees. Serves 4 to 6.

Roast Pork Loin

1	pork loin roast	1	teaspoon black pepper
1	tablespoon salt	1	teaspoon thyme
1	tablespoon paprika	1/2	teaspoon nutmeg

Tie roast to create an even thickness. Mix all spices together. Rub spice mixture on meat and wrap roast in plastic and refrigerate for at least 2 hours or up to 24 hours. Adjust rack to center of oven and heat oven to 475 degrees. Place meat on rack set in shallow roasting pan. Roast exactly 30 minutes. Remove meat from oven; immediately reduce oven temperature to 325 degrees. Let roast rest at room temperature, tented, for 30 minutes. Return meat to oven and roast until meat thermometer inserted in thickest part of roast reaches an internal temperature of 155 degrees. Let roast stand at room temperature tented for 15 to 20 minutes to finish cooking. Slice meat thin and serve. It will be a little pink and tender.

Tenderloin of Pork Nuveau

PORK

½ cup honey
¼ cup hoisin sauce
    (found in the oriental
    section of the store)
¼ cup soy sauce

1 tablespoon minced elephant
    garlic
1-2 pork tenderloins
    (most tenderloins are
    packaged with 2)
2 tablespoons butter

SAUCE

1 cup heavy cream

¼ cup blue cheese

Combine all ingredients except pork mixing well. (honey, hoisin, soy sauce, garlic, and melted butter). Pour mixture over pork in a glass dish, cover and marinate over night in the refrigerator. Turn once or twice while marinating. Turn meat often while grilling. Do not put over red coals, the honey will char over extreme heat. Normal sized tenderloin can take 18 to 30 minutes to grill. Wood chips add flavor. For Sauce: Combine cream and cheese in saucepan over moderate heat. Reduce until thickened and cheese has melted. Do not boil. Serve sauce over meat or on the side.

Sunday Pork Roast

3-4 pound pork loin roast
    Salt and pepper to taste
    Garlic powder to taste
½ cup apricot nectar
½ cup port wine
3 onions, quartered

¼ cup white raisins
1 tablespoon soy sauce
1 tablespoon brown sugar
½ teaspoon ginger
¼ teaspoon marjoram

Soak clay baking pot for 10 to 15 minutes in cold water. Salt, pepper and garlic powder roast to taste. Combine remaining ingredients in jar and shake well. Pour mixture over roast. Cover with lid and place in a cold oven. Bake at 425 degrees for 2 hours. Bake 2½ hours if roast has a bone in it.

Cajun Ham Steak

2   teaspoons Cajun seasoning
     blend
½   teaspoon sugar
1   (20 ounces) fully cooked
     smoked ham steak, ½ inch
     thick

Lime wedges
Fresh cilantro sprigs for
 garnish

Heat ridge grill pan or heavy skillet over medium-high heat until very hot but not smoking. In a small bowl combine Cajun seasoning and sugar. Rub mixture on both sides of ham steak. Place ham steak in skillet and cook until heated through and lightly browned, about 4 minutes on each side.

Black-Eyed Pea Supper Dish

2   (16 ounce) cans black-eyed
     peas
1   pound ground sausage
1   cup chopped green pepper
½   cup chopped onion
2   garlic cloves, finely chopped

2   cups canned tomatoes
     chopped
½   teaspoon black pepper
½   teaspoon oregano
½   teaspoon rosemary
1   cup grated cheese

Cook sausage in large frying pan, crumbling with a fork as it cooks. Drain fat from pan. Add green pepper, onion, and garlic. Cook 5 minutes stirring pepper and onion into sausage. Add tomatoes and seasonings and stir well. Pour in black-eyed peas with the liquid in the can. Cover and simmer slowly for 15 minutes. Serve very hot with grated cheese sprinkled on top.

Sausage Lasagna

SAUCE

- 3 tablespoons olive oil, divided
- 1 pound sweet Italian sausages, casings removed
- 2 ounces sliced prosciutto, chopped
- 2 cups chopped onion
- 1 celery stalk, chopped
- 3 cloves garlic, chopped
- 1 teaspoon dried oregano
- ¼ teaspoon dried crushed red pepper
- 1 can tomato paste
- 1 (28 ounce) can Italian tomatoes in purée
- 2 tablespoons fresh basil, chopped

LASAGNA

- 12 lasagna noodles, cooked
- 1 (15 ounce) container whole milk ricotta cheese
- 4 cups shredded mozzarella cheese

Heat 1 tablespoon oil in large saucepan over medium-high heat. Add sausage. Sauté until browned, breaking up with fork. Add prosciutto. Stir for 1 minute. Transfer to a bowl. Heat 2 tablespoons of oil in same pan over medium-high heat. Add onions, celery, garlic, oregano and red pepper. Sauté until tender (about 5 minutes). Stir in tomato paste. Add tomatoes, basil and reserved sausage mixture. Season with salt and pepper to taste.

To cook pasta: cook noodles in boiling salted water until tender but still firm to the bite. Drain and arrange on baking sheet (single layer) until ready to use. Mix ricotta cheese and 1½ cups mozzarella cheese in bowl. Season with salt and pepper to taste. Mix in egg. Brush 13 x 9 inch baking dish with oil. Spread 1 cup sauce on bottom of pan. Arrange 3 noodles atop sauce. Spread ¼ cup cheese mixture over noodles. Spoon 1½ cups sauce on top. Repeat with noodles, cheese and sauce 2 more times. Cover with 3 noodles. Cover top with remaining cheese.

Bake, covered, 40 minutes in a 350 degrees oven. Uncover and bake until heated through, about 15 minutes. Let stand 10 minutes before serving.

The Best Ribs Ever

Reynolds Hot Bag
Pork or Beef ribs

Barbeque sauce
Small onion

Open the oven bag and spray with cooking spray. Place ribs in the bag. Cut up the onion and place inside bag. Pour entire bottle of barbeque sauce over the ribs. Stir softly, not to puncture bag. Bake at 200 degrees for 3 or more hours. They will fall apart as you take them out.

Party Shrimp Supreme

1 (4 ounce) can button mushrooms
¼ cup slivered almonds
1 small green pepper cut into 1 inch strips
¼ cup melted butter
2 tablespoons orange juice
1 teaspoon lemon juice or 3 tablespoons dry white wine

2 (10¾ ounce) cans cream of mushroom soup
½ teaspoon celery salt
¼ cup sliced black olives
¼ cup chopped pimento
2 tablespoons dried chopped parsley
   Dash Tabasco sauce
2 pounds peeled shrimp

Drain mushrooms and reserve liquid. Sauté mushrooms and almonds in butter. Add mushroom liquid, lemon juice or wine, and orange juice. When hot, add soup and celery salt and blend well. Add olives, green pepper, pimento, parsley, and Tabasco sauce. A few minutes before serving, add peeled shrimp and cook until shrimp are pink. Do not boil. This dish will impress when served over hot, white rice with a side salad and bread.

Greek Style Scampi

1	teaspoon olive oil	1¼	pounds large shrimp, peeled and de-veined
5	cloves garlic, minced	1	cup crumbled feta cheese
½	cup chopped fresh parsley, divided	2	tablespoons fresh lemon juice
3½	cups seeded and chopped fresh tomatoes or 2 (28 ounce) cans chopped tomatoes, drained	¼	teaspoon freshly ground pepper
		4	cups hot cooked angel hair pasta

Preheat oven to 400 degrees. Heat oil in large Dutch oven over medium heat. Add garlic; sauté 30 seconds. Add ¼ cup parsley and tomatoes. Reduce heat and simmer 10 minutes. Add shrimp and cook 5 minutes. Pour mixture into baking dish and sprinkle with cheese. Bake for 10 minutes. Sprinkle with remaining parsley, lemon juice and pepper. Serve over pasta.

Shrimp and Grits

4	cups water	6	slices bacon, chopped
	Salt and pepper to taste	4	teaspoons lemon juice
1	cup stone ground grits	2	tablespoons chopped parsley
3	tablespoons butter	1	cup thinly sliced scallions
2	cups shredded Cheddar cheese	1	large clove garlic, minced
1	pound shrimp, peeled and deveined	⅓	cup fresh red pepper, chopped

Bring water to boil and add salt and pepper. Add grits and cook until water is absorbed, about 20 to 25 minutes. Remove from heat and stir in butter and cheese. Rinse shrimp and pat dry. Fry bacon in a large skillet until browned, drain well. In grease, add shrimp and cook until pink. Add lemon juice, chopped bacon, parsley, scallions, garlic and red pepper for 3 minutes. Spoon grits into a serving bowl, add shrimp mixture and mix well. Serve immediately.

Shrimp Grits with Country Ham and Gravy

HAM

1	tablespoon butter
3	ounces country ham, chopped
2	ounces mushroom caps

¼	cup chopped green onions
½	cup Madeira wine
½	cup strong coffee

GRAVY

6	ounces V-8 juice
1	tablespoon cornstarch

1	tablespoon thyme

SHRIMP

2	tablespoons butter
2	tablespoons chopped green pepper
2	pounds medium shrimp, cleaned

1¼	teaspoons hot chili sauce
½	cup fresh parsley
	Grits, prepared to your liking

Sauté ham in butter. Brown mushrooms and onion. Add Madeira and coffee; simmer 15 minutes to reduce by one half.

Dissolve cornstarch in vegetable juice and add thyme.

Sauté shrimp in butter with green pepper. Add the chili sauce and parsley. Serve over cheese grits or garlic cheese grits.

Shrimp Fettuccine Alfredo

3 pounds large shrimp
1 stick butter
4 tablespoons minced garlic
1 pound fettuccini pasta, cooked
1 small onion, diced
1 (8 ounce) package mushrooms
1/3 cup flour
3 cups milk
2 cups half-and-half
3/4 cup fresh grated Romano cheese
1/2 cup fresh grated Parmesan cheese
1/2 cup ricotta cheese (whole milk)
1/2 cup sour cream
1 cup mozzarella cheese
Salt and pepper to taste

Peel and devein shrimp. Boil 2 minutes. Remove from water. Melt 3 tablespoons butter. Sauté shrimp and 2 tablespoons garlic for 5 minutes. Set aside. Melt 2 to 3 tablespoons butter, and then sauté mushrooms, onion, and 2 tablespoons garlic. Add flour to make a thick paste. Slowly whisk in half-and-half and milk, stirring to thicken. Add the Romano, Parmesan, ricotta, and mozzarella cheeses, along with the sour cream. Stir constantly until melted. Add shrimp mixture. Season to taste with salt and pepper. Serve over pasta. Makes 8 servings.

Coquille St. Jacques

6 tablespoons butter, divided
3 tablespoons flour
1 teaspoon salt
1/2 teaspoon white pepper
2 cups light cream
1/2 pound sea scallops, halved
1/4 cup finely chopped onion
1/2 cup sliced mushrooms
1/4 pound cooked shrimp
1/4 pound white lump crabmeat
2 tablespoons cooking sherry
Parsley
3 tablespoons bread crumbs

In double boiler top, melt 4 tablespoons butter, blend in flour, salt and pepper on high. Gradually add cream, stirring constantly, bringing to a boil. Return top to double boiler and cook 5 more minutes. Melt remaining butter in skillet. Add scallops, mushrooms, shrimp, crabmeat and sherry. Mix lightly. Spoon into 6 ramekins. Chop parsley into bread crumbs and mix. Sprinkle crumb mixture over each dish. Bake at 400 degrees for 10 minutes or until evenly browned. Serve immediately. Serves 6.

Crab Cakes

1	pound fresh picked crabmeat	½	cup mayonnaise
1	cup cooked corn	½	teaspoon dried mustard
½	cup finely diced onion	½	teaspoon cayenne pepper
½	cup finely diced green bell pepper		Fresh ground pepper and salt
½	cup finely diced red bell pepper	1	egg, lightly beaten
½	cup finely diced celery	3	cups bread or cracker crumbs

Combine crabmeat, corn, onion, peppers and celery in mixing bowl and toss well. In another bowl combine mayonnaise with mustard and cayenne and stir into crabmeat mixture, adding salt and pepper to taste. Using a rubber spatula, gently fold in the eggs and bread crumbs. Form into cakes and dip back into crumb mixture. Sauté in oil and butter until golden brown.

Tulla White, Owner/Chef The Basil Leaf, Venucci, Tulla's Bayou Bar and Grill and Tulla White Cuisine and Catering.

Key West Crab Cakes with Mustard Sauce

CAKES

1	pound crabmeat	2	eggs
1	tablespoon small diced red bell pepper	1	tablespoon baking powder
1	tablespoon small diced green bell pepper	1	tablespoon Worcestershire sauce
1	fine chopped fresh parsley	1½	teaspoons crab seasoning
1	mayonnaise	2	tablespoons canola oil

SAUCE

¼	cup mayonnaise	¼	cup lemon juice
¼	cup Dijon mustard		

In a large bowl, mix all ingredients, except oil and mustard sauce. Heat oil in large skillet over medium-high heat. With a tablespoon, carefully spoon mixture (mini cakes) into the pan. They will be loose at first. Cook 2 minutes per side. Mix mustard sauce ingredients together and serve with crab cakes.

Cumin Coriander Rubbed Salmon with Mango Peach Salsa

SALMON

1	salmon filet for each guest	1	tablespoon cumin seeds
1	tablespoon coriander seeds	¼	tablespoon kosher salt

MANGO PEACH SALSA

1	mango, peeled, diced	1	red pepper, diced
3	peaches, peeled, diced	3	scallions, sliced
1	jalapeño pepper, diced		Juice of 3 limes
1	Vidalia onion, chopped		

Remove skin and bones from each filet, and cut each filet crosswise. Grind spices in a spice grinder or coffee bean grinder. Rub onto salmon filets. Let marinate 1 to 4 hours. Bake uncovered at 350 degrees approximately 10 minutes or until opaque. Combine all salsa ingredients and spoon over ⅓ of cooked salmon. Makes 6 to 8 servings.

Maple Grilled Salmon

¼	cup maple syrup	¼	teaspoon ground ginger
1	tablespoon lemon juice	1¼	pound salmon fillet
2	tablespoons light soy sauce	2	thinly sliced green onions
1	teaspoon Dijon mustard		

Mix all ingredients except salmon and onions. Cut salmon into four planks and place in shallow baking dish. Drizzle marinade over fish reserving some to serve with fish. Refrigerate about 30 minutes and grill over medium fire for 10 to 15 minutes or until fish flakes easily with fork. To serve, drizzle reserved marinade over fish and top with green onions.

Salmon is a perfect low-calorie source for many essential nutrients.

Fresh Salmon Cakes

CAKES

2	tablespoons butter	2	eggs, lightly beaten
¼	cup sliced green onion	3	tablespoons cream
1	clove garlic, minced	¼	cup fresh slivered basil
1	pound cooked salmon	½	teaspoon salt
1	cup homemade bread crumbs	¼	teaspoon pepper
		2	tablespoons olive oil

TOMATO BASIL SAUCE, OPTIONAL

⅓	cup white wine	2	tablespoons cream
2	tablespoons finely chopped shallots	½	cup chilled butter
		¼	cup fresh chopped basil
1	teaspoon white wine vinegar	¼	teaspoon salt
2	teaspoons tomato paste		Pinch white pepper

For the cakes, melt butter in small sauté pan over medium low heat. Add green onion and cook 2 minutes. Transfer to bowl. Add all remaining ingredients except oil and blend. Refrigerate, covered for 30 minutes. Form 8 cakes and cook in olive oil for 3 minutes per side.

For sauce, combine wine, shallot, vinegar and tomato paste in small saucepan. Bring to boil over medium-high heat and reduce to 2 tablespoons. Add cream and boil 1 minute. Reduce heat to medium and add cold butter 1 tablespoon at a time. Whisk constantly until all butter is added and sauce has thickened. Do not let it boil again. Remove from heat and stir in basil, salt and pepper. Reheat before serving over cakes.

Tilapia with Lemon Butter Sauce

TILAPIA

3	teaspoons flour	1½	pounds tilapia fillets
1	teaspoon seasoned salt	2	tablespoons butter

LEMON BUTTER SAUCE

1	tablespoon butter	2	tablespoons fresh Italian
1	teaspoon flour		parsley
¼	cup white wine		Juice of 1 lemon

Place 3 teaspoons flour and seasoned salt in a large zip-top bag. Shake to mix and set aside. Rinse parsley and lemon. Remove stems from parsley, coarsely chop leaves, then measure. Slice lemon in half. Set both aside. Preheat large sauté pan on medium-high heat for 2 to 3 minutes. Rinse fish. Check for bones by pressing on fillet and removing all bones. Add fish and cook 3 minutes. Add 1 tablespoon butter to center of pan. Using spatula, turn fillets over distributing butter under each fillet. Cook 3 more minutes until fish is golden and flakes easily. Place fish on serving plates. Place 1 tablespoon butter, 1 teaspoon flour, wine and juice of lemon in sauté pan. Heat for 1 to 2 minutes until thickened, stirring occasionally. Stir parsley into butter sauce and serve over fish. Yields 4 servings.

Dill Sauce

½ **teaspoon dill weed**
½ **teaspoon cream of tarter**

½ **teaspoon lemon or lime juice**
½ **cup mayonnaise**

Combine all ingredients and use as a rub for fish. Can also be used as a side sauce during meal.

Tennessee River White BBQ Sauce

2 **cups mayonnaise**
2 **tablespoons freshly ground black pepper**
2 **tablespoons coarse salt**

6 **tablespoons lemon juice**
6 **tablespoons cider, white or red wine vinegar**
4 **tablespoons refined sugar**

Mix all ingredients well. Makes 3 cups.

Try these variations to your taste: add more or less mayonnaise for thicker or thinner sauce, add water for weaker sauce, add more (but never less) pepper, or add less or no sugar. This tangy basting and dipping sauce originates from North Alabama and is used primarily with chicken, pork chops or ribs.

Kerri Vice, Owner/Chef Table Toppers Catering Co.

Hot and Sweet Dipping Sauce

½ cup rice wine vinegar
½ cup sugar
1-2 cloves garlic, chopped

¼ teaspoon salt
1½ teaspoons dried red pepper
  flakes

Heat vinegar in saucepan to a boil. Add sugar and stir. Reduce heat to simmer and cook for 5 minutes on low. Stir in garlic, salt and pepper flakes. Cool over ice-water bath. Store in glass jar in refrigerator up to 2 days.

Jamie Keating, Owner/Chef Gourmet Events

Shallots Caper Tarter Sauce

2 cups mayonnaise
4 tablespoons fresh lemon
  juice
2 teaspoons Worcestershire
  sauce
1 tablespoon Tabasco sauce

½ cup finely diced dill pickle
½ cup chopped fresh parsley
4 tablespoons finely mixed
  shallots
4 tablespoons capers
  Fresh ground pepper and salt

Mix the first 4 ingredients in a bowl. Fold in the rest of the ingredients, seasoning with salt and pepper. Refrigerate.

Tulla White, Owner/Chef The Basil Leaf, Venucci, Tulla's Bayou Bar and Grill and Tulla White Cuisine and Catering.

Make your own seasoning

Five Spice Powder

1 teaspoon ground cinnamon	1 teaspoon star anise
1 teaspoon ground cloves	1 teaspoon Szechwan
1 teaspoon fennel seed	peppercorns

Great for salads or as part of marinating/ rubbing meat.

Italian Herb Seasoning

1 teaspoon oregano	1 teaspoon basil
1 teaspoon marjoram	1 teaspoon rosemary
1 teaspoon thyme	1 teaspoon sage

Use this with your favorite chili recipe!

Chili Powder

3 tablespoons paprika	1 teaspoon cayenne pepper
1 tablespoon ground cumin	½ teaspoon garlic powder
2 tablespoons oregano	

This is great on a French bread loaf or tossed with chips.

House Blend

1 teaspoon garlic powder	¼ teaspoon cayenne pepper
1 teaspoon dried thyme	¼ teaspoon Kosher salt
¼ teaspoon paprika	

Breads and
Breakfast

VILLAGE LIFE

MILL WOMEN TAKE CHARGE

During the World War II era, many Troup County women were not only bread bakers – but also bread winners. The local textile industry had always put food on the table, as well as provided a source of social and educational development. Mill houses, churches, schools, theaters, parks, greenhouses and other amenities were built along with the mills. At the center of these mill villages were strong and determined, yet caring women.

When Troup County's men went off to war, wives, mothers and daughters were left to take charge. Women workers were popping up in every industry including the textile mills, which also made materials in support of the war. These women were doing the jobs of the men who were off fighting, while still cooking, cleaning and raising their children. This was a time when it was safe to put the children to bed in the mill house, which was paid for through a paycheck deduction, and report for work on the third shift beginning at 10 p.m. If there was a noise in the night while mom was working at the mill, children often went to a neighbor's home for comforting.

Life in the mill villages was not always easy, but it was much better than farming, which afforded little social benefits and activities. Thanks to the generosity of mills like Dunson and Callaway, employees and their families enjoyed nice homes and schools. Led by strong women, Troup County's mill villages offered a real sense of community. Today, the memories live on in the hearts of many Troup County women, who are quick to share their stories of growing up in a mill village.

Breads & Breakfast

Antipasta Bread

1 (6½ ounce) can artichoke hearts
⅓ cup pepperoni, sliced into small pieces
½ cup sliced black olives
2 cloves fresh garlic, pressed
¼ cup butter, melted
6 ounces grated Parmesan cheese
2 packages refrigerated dinner rolls

Preheat oven to 375 degrees. Spray Bundt pan with cooking spray. Mix first 4 ingredients together and set aside. Slice the dinner rolls into about 32 pieces. Roll each of the first 10 pieces in butter and then cheese. Place the pieces in the bottom of the pan. Spread one half of the set aside mixture over this layer. Roll 10 to 12 bread pieces in butter and cheese. Spread remaining mixture over this. Roll the remaining bread pieces in butter and cheese. Place on top of other layers. Bake 27 to 30 minutes. Remove from the oven and let stand for 5 minutes before inverting onto platter. Serve warm.

Cranberry-Apple Casserole

3 cups peeled, chopped apples
2½ cups fresh cranberries, divided
2 tablespoons all-purpose flour
1 cup sugar
3 (1.625 ounce) packages instant oatmeal with cinnamon and spice
¾ cup chopped pecans
½ cup all-purpose flour
½ cup firmly packed brown sugar
½ cup melted butter
Pecan halves

Combine apples, 2 cups cranberries, and 2 tablespoons flour, tossing to coat. Add 1 cup sugar, mixing well. Place in a 2 quart casserole dish. Combine oatmeal, chopped pecans, ½ cup flour, and brown sugar. Add butter and stir well. Spoon over fruit mixture. Bake uncovered at 350 degrees for 45 minutes. Garnish with pecan halves and the rest of the cranberries. Makes 6 to 8 servings.

Banana Sour Cream Coffee Cake

½ cup chopped nuts
1¼ cups sugar, divided
½ teaspoon cinnamon
½ cup shortening
2 eggs
1 cup mashed banana

1 teaspoon vanilla extract
½ cup sour cream
2 cups all-purpose flour
1 teaspoon baking powder
1 teaspoon baking soda
¼ teaspoon salt

Combine nuts, ¼ cup sugar and cinnamon. Stir well and set aside. Combine shortening and 1 cup sugar. Cream until light and fluffy. Beat in eggs, bananas and vanilla. Stir in sour cream. Combine remaining dry ingredients separately. Add to creamed mixture. Stir just enough to blend. Sprinkle half of reserved cinnamon mixture into bottom of well-greased 10 inch Bundt pan. Spoon half of batter into pan. Sprinkle remaining mixture over batter and spoon remaining batter on top. Bake at 350 degrees for 40 to 45 minutes. Cool cake 5 minutes on wire rack. Invert onto serving plate and serve hot.

If you're looking for an alternative to banana bread, this is your recipe. It consistently turns out great.

Cinnamon Logs

1	(16 ounce) loaf thinly sliced bread	½	cup powdered sugar
1	(8 ounce) package cream cheese	½	cup melted butter
1	egg white	1	cup sugar
		1	tablespoon cinnamon

Cut the crusts off the bread and discard. Mix cream cheese, egg white and powdered sugar together until smooth. Spread mixture generously on each slice of bread. Roll each slice into a log shape. Dip each into melted butter. Mix sugar and cinnamon together and roll each log into this mixture. Bake at 350 degrees for 15 minutes or until lightly golden. To serve, leave the pieces in log shape or cut in half to form bite-sized pieces.

Cinnamon Nut Coffee Cake

CAKE

1	stick butter, melted	2	shakes ground cloves
1	teaspoon vanilla	1½	tablespoons grated orange peel
2	(10 count) cans butter biscuits	4	ounces cream cheese (cut into cubes)
1	cup granulated sugar	½	cup chopped nuts
2	shakes ground cinnamon		

GLAZE

1	cup powdered sugar	2	teaspoons orange juice

Preheat oven to 350 degrees. Grease or spray Bundt pan. Melt butter and add vanilla. In separate bowl, mix sugar, nuts, cinnamon, cloves and orange peel. Separate a biscuit and put a small cube of cream cheese in middle and seal the sides of the biscuit. Dip in melted butter, dredge in bowl of dry ingredients. Stand on side in pan. Bake for 35 minutes. Turn out on wire rack and put on plate. Mix glaze and pour over warm bread to serve.

Corn and Jalapeño Waffles

Cooking spray	2 cups low-fat buttermilk
1¾ cups all-purpose flour	1 tablespoon vegetable oil
2 teaspoons baking powder	1 large egg
1 teaspoon ground cumin	½ cup jalapeño pepper, minced
½ teaspoon baking soda	1 (11 ounce) can whole-kernel
½ teaspoon salt	corn, drained

Coat a waffle iron with cooking spray and preheat. Lightly spoon the flour into dry measuring cups and level with a knife. Combine flour and next 4 ingredients in a large bowl. Place buttermilk, oil and egg in a medium bowl and stir well with a whisk. Add buttermilk mixture into flour mixture and stir until smooth. Fold in jalapeño and corn. Spoon about ½ cup batter onto hot waffle iron, spreading batter to edges. Cook 3 to 5 minutes or until done. These are an alternative to cornbread. Serve with butter, salsa or jalapeño jelly.

Sea Island Cornbread

1 cup self-rising cornmeal	1 cup sour cream
¾ cup self-rising flour	1¼ cups grated cheese
¾ cup vegetable oil, divided	¼ cup chopped onion, optional
1 (8 ounce) can cream style	¼ cup chopped green pepper,
corn	optional
2 eggs	

Preheat oven to 375 degrees. Place ¼ cup oil into a cast iron skillet and put in the oven for 5 minutes. Mix all ingredients together and pour into skillet. Bake until golden brown, about 30 minutes. Serves 8.

If you prefer soft cornbread, coat with butter immediately upon removing from oven.

Both of these recipes are delicious with chicken and pork dishes as well as with salads.

Short Bread

1½ sticks butter	2 teaspoons grated orange zest
1¼ cups sugar	
2 egg yolks	4 cups sifted all-purpose flour
2 tablespoons Amaretto	Salt

Cream butter and sugar together until mixture is light and fluffy. Add yolks and beat well. Scrape down the sides of the bowl and add the Amaretto and orange zest, mix well. Slowly add the flour and a pinch of salt. Mix just until a heavy dough forms. Press the dough evenly into a greased 9 x 13 inch pan. Bake at 325 degrees until golden brown, about 35 to 40 minutes. Cool slightly and cut into desired shapes.

Robert Standard, Owner/Chef Kazan

Cranberry Nut Bread

2 cups plain flour	1 tablespoon grated orange rind
1 cup sugar	
1½ teaspoons baking powder	1 egg, beaten
½ teaspoon salt	½ cup chopped pecans
½ teaspoon baking soda	1 cup fresh cranberries, chopped
¼ cup shortening	
¾ cup orange juice	

Sift dry ingredients together. Cut in shortening until mixture resembles cornmeal. Combine orange juice, rind and egg and add to dry mixture. Mix just until flour is dampened. Fold in nuts and cranberries. Pour in greased and floured loaf pan. Bake at 350 degrees for 1 hour.

Berry French Toast

TOAST

- 1 loaf French bread, cut into 1 inch cubes
- 2 (8 ounce) packages cream cheese, cut into 1 inch cubes
- 1 cup raspberries or blueberries
- 12 large eggs
- ⅓ cup maple syrup
- 2 cups milk

BERRY SAUCE

- 1 cup sugar
- 2 tablespoons cornstarch
- 1 cup water
- 1 cup berries
- 1 tablespoon butter

For toast, arrange half of bread cubes in greased 9 x 13 inch pan. Scatter cream cheese on top and then berries. Cover with remaining cubes. Beat eggs, milk and syrup in bowl. Pour over bread mixture. Cover with foil sprayed with cooking spray and chill overnight. Bake covered at 350 degrees for 45 minutes. Uncover and bake an additional 30 minutes or until puffed and golden.

For sauce, mix sugar, water and cornstarch. Cook over medium-high heat, stirring occasionally, for 5 minutes or until thick. Add berries and simmer for 10 minutes. Add butter and stir until melted. Cut French toast into 8 to 10 pieces and serve topped with sauce.

Karen Scarborough, Owner/Chef Thyme Away Bed and Breakfast

Try using both raspberries and blueberries or try a different flavor syrup.

Dutch Babies with Fresh Fruit

2 tablespoons butter
½ cup all-purpose flour
¼ teaspoon fresh grated
   nutmeg
   Salt
2 eggs

½ cup milk
Fruit of choice
Powdered sugar
Vanilla yogurt
Nutmeg as garnish

Melt butter in 9 to 10 inch glass pie pan in 425 degrees oven. Mix milk and eggs together and add flour, pinch of salt and nutmeg. Leave a bit lumpy. Pour mixture into pie pan and bake for 15 to 20 minutes until brown and crispy. Fill with fresh fruit and top with powdered sugar, vanilla yogurt and nutmeg.

Karen Scarborough, Owner/Chef Thyme Away Bed and Breakfast

Mary's German Pancakes

   Vegetable oil
3 eggs
¾ cup milk
¾ cup all-purpose flour
   Salt

1 lemon
   Fruit spread or applesauce
2 tablespoons butter
   Cinnamon sugar

Heat ⅛ inch oil in 9 inch cast iron skillet in 425 degrees oven. Mix eggs, milk, flour and pinch of salt and pour into hot pan. Bake 15 to 18 minutes until puffed and brown. Remove pancake from pan and place on platter. Turn oven down to warm setting. Drizzle pancake with juice of 1 lemon. Spread pancake with desired filling and roll up jelly roll fashion. Pour butter over pancake and sprinkle with sugar. Place on baking sheet in oven for about 10 minutes. Slice and serve.

Karen Scarborough, Owner/Chef Thyme Away Bed and Breakfast

French Toast Soufflé

12	slices white bread, crust removed	2	cup half-and-half
2	(8 ounce) packages cream cheese	½	cup maple syrup
12	large eggs	½	teaspoon maple extract
		½	teaspoon vanilla extract
		3	tablespoons powdered sugar

Spray 13 x 9 inch baking dish with cooking spray. Place 8 bread slices in bottom of dish. Place remaining 4 slices down the center, creating a second layer. Beat cream cheese and eggs until well mixed and frothy. Add additional ingredients and stir. Pour egg mixture over bread. Cover and refrigerate overnight.

To bake: remove casserole from refrigerator and let stand at room temperature for 30 minutes. Bake at 350 degrees for 50 to 60 minutes. To check doneness, insert knife in center. Soufflé should be glistening but not "eggie". Sift powdered sugar on top and serve with maple sugar. Serves 12 to 14.

Brown 1 pound mild pork sausage and crumble between layers or add ¼ teaspoon dried mustard to ingredients. Also, before baking place 12 dollops of strawberry jam on top. One more variation is to place 14 to 16 cooked bacon slices between bread layers.

Lemon Bread

When Taste of Lemon first opened; each table was served this bread. As business grew, it was impossible to make enough bread each day to keep up with demand. To this day, customers still ask about the lemon bread they remember being served.

BREAD

1²/₃ cups plain flour, sifted
½ teaspoon salt
1 teaspoon baking powder
½ cup butter, softened
1 cup sugar

2 eggs, slightly beaten
½ cup milk
2 lemons, grated rinds of each (use the juice below)

GLAZE

¼ cup sugar

Juice of 2 lemons

Sift together flour, salt and baking powder. In a separate bowl, cream butter and sugar until fluffy. Add eggs. Alternately, add flour mixture and milk to the butter mixture, ending with the flour mixture. Beating constantly, stir in lemon rind. Pour into greased 9 x 5 inch loaf pan. Line pan with wax paper to prevent sticking. Bake at 350 degrees for 1 hour or until firm. Don't overcook!

Mix ingredients of glaze together. Prick the bread with a toothpick and pour on glaze. Remove bread from the pan after it has cooled about 10 minutes. Don't let it stay too long in the pan or it will not come out easily. Allow to cool out of the pan before slicing.

Betty Daniel, Owner/Chef Taste of Lemon

Lemon Pull Aparts

ROLLS

2	lemon rinds, grated
½	cup sugar

12	Marie's dinner rolls, thawed but still cold
¼	cup butter, melted

CITRUS GLAZE

1	cup powdered sugar
1	tablespoon butter, melted

2	tablespoons fresh lemon juice

Mix grated lemon rind with sugar. Cut rolls in half and place in a 12 inch deep dish pizza pan or 9 x 13 inch baking pan sprayed with non-stick cooking spray. Drizzle melted butter over rolls. Sprinkle with ½ lemon rind/sugar mixture. Cover with plastic wrap sprayed with non-stick cooking spray. Let rise until double in size. Remove wrap. Sprinkle on remaining lemon rind/sugar mixture. Bake at 350 degrees for 20 to 25 minutes. Remove immediately from pan and place on cooling rack. To make glaze, combine powdered sugar, butter and lemon juice. Mix well. Drizzle glaze over rolls. Serve warm. Makes 12 servings.

Magic Marshmallow Crescent Puffs

PUFFS

¼ cup sugar
1 teaspoon cinnamon
2 (8 ounce) cans refrigerated
   quick dinner rolls

16 large marshmallows
¼ cup butter, melted

GLAZE

½ cup powdered sugar
2 teaspoons milk

½ teaspoon vanilla
¼ cup chopped nuts, optional

Heat oven to 375 degrees. Combine sugar and cinnamon. Separate crescent dough into 16 triangles. Dip a marshmallow in melted butter, roll in a sugar and cinnamon mixture. Place marshmallow on shortest side of triangle. Fold corners over marshmallow and pinching edges of dough to seal. Dip in melted margarine and place margarine side down in deep muffin cup. Repeat with remaining marshmallows. Place pan on foil or cookie sheet during baking to guard against spillage. Bake at 375 degrees for 10 to 15 minutes or until golden brown. Immediately remove from pans. To make glaze, combine all ingredients, drizzle over warm rolls and sprinkle with nuts. Makes 16 rolls.

Orange Nutty Coffee Cake

¾ **cup sugar**
½ **cup finely chopped pecans**
2 **teaspoons grated orange rind**
4 **ounces cream cheese**
2 **cans buttermilk biscuits**

½ **cup butter, melted**
1 **cup powdered sugar**
2 **tablespoons fresh orange
   juice**

Combine first 3 ingredients and set aside. Place 1 teaspoon cream cheese in center of each biscuit, fold over and pinch edges to seal. Dip biscuits in melted butter, then dredge in sugar mixture. Place curved side down in a lightly greased Bundt pan. Drizzle any remaining butter over biscuits. Bake at 350 degrees until golden brown, about 35 minutes. Immediately invert onto serving plate. Combine powdered sugar and orange juice. Drizzle over cake and serve warm. Makes 8 to 10 servings.

If you are looking for any easy, tasty gift, this is your best bet.

Pumpkin Bread

3⅓ **cups all-purpose flour**
3 **cups sugar**
½ **teaspoon salt**
1½ **teaspoons cinnamon**
1 **teaspoon nutmeg**

2 **teaspoons baking soda**
1 **cup oil**
⅔ **cup water**
4 **eggs, slightly beaten**
1 **(16 ounce) can pumpkin
   purée**

Sift dry ingredients together. Form well in center. Add remaining ingredients and mix until smooth. Pour into 3 well-greased loaf pans (or 8 mini-loaf pans). Bake for 1 hour at 350 degrees.

Orange Sweet Rolls

ROLLS

1	cup scalded milk, cooled to lukewarm	½	cup sugar
1	package dry yeast	3	eggs
3	tablespoons soft butter	½	teaspoon salt
		4½-5	cups sifted flour, divided

FILLING

6	tablespoons soft butter	½	cup sugar
1½	teaspoons grated orange peel		

GLAZE

2	cups powdered sugar		Salt
2-4	tablespoons orange juice		vanilla extract

For rolls, mix first 4 ingredients and let stand 5 minutes. Add eggs, salt and 1 cup of flour and beat well. Mix in 3½ to 4 more cups flour to make a soft dough. Knead on floured board 10 minutes. Kneading can be done with dough hook on electric mixer. Round up in a greased bowl turning greased side up. Cover with plastic wrap and let rise 2 hours or until doubled. Punch down and divide dough in half. Roll each half into an 8 x 10 inch rectangle. Mix filling ingredients together and leaving ½ inch clear along one long side, spread each rectangle with the mixture. Rollup from 1 long side, jelly-roll fashion, with the clear edges last so it will stick together. Place on a cookie sheet and freeze about 15 minutes to make cutting easier. Cut each long roll into 18 slices. Place in buttered pan, barely touching. Cover and let rise about 1 hour. Bake at 375 degrees for 15 minutes. Mix glaze ingredients together with pinch of salt and a few drops of vanilla. Cool rolls slightly and glaze.

The exact amount of flour needed varies with the humidity. These may be wrapped and frozen after baking and cooling, but before glazing. Allow to thaw wrapped, then uncover and warm 15 minutes in a 300 degrees oven before glazing.

Baked Sour Cream Omelet

6	slices Texas toast bread	6	eggs
4	ounces grated Gruyère cheese	2	cups milk
4	ounces grated Monterey Jack cheese	¾	cup sour cream
		1	tablespoon Dijon mustard
12	slices bacon cooked crisp and crumbled	⅓-½	cup grated Parmesan cheese
			Paprika

Spray 9 x 13 inch pan with cooking spray. Place single layer of bread in the pan and top with Gruyère, Monterey Jack and bacon. Combine eggs, milk, sour cream and mustard. Pour over the bread, cover and chill overnight. Bake covered in 350 degrees oven for 30 minutes. Uncover, sprinkle Parmesan and paprika on top and continue baking for 30 more minutes. When done, the omelet should be puffed up and a knife inserted should come out clean. Serve hot.

Karen Scarborough, Owner/Chef Thyme Away Bed and Breakfast

You can substitute the bacon for packaged bacon found in the salad section of your local grocery store. This dish is also good reheated.

Cheese Soufflé

1	(1 pound) day old challah loaf
1	dozen eggs
1	stick butter, melted

1-1½	pounds grated Cheddar cheese
½	teaspoon powdered mustard
1	teaspoon salt
1	quart milk

Cut crust from bread, slice into 14 pieces and cube. In mixer combine eggs, butter, mustard and salt. Blend well then add milk. Spray 3 quart casserole dish with non-stick cooking spray. Place layers of bread in dish and then cheese. Repeat using all bread and cheese. Pour egg mixture over this. Cover and refrigerate overnight. Remove from refrigerator 1½ hours before baking. Bake at 400 degrees for 15 minutes. Reduce oven to 375 degrees and continue cooking until done, about 1 hour to 1 hour 15 minutes.

Kerri Vice, Owner/Chef Table Toppers Catering Co.

Your local bakery can make challah for you and slice it as well; use extra sharp Cheddar cheese if you prefer. Plan to serve this dish for breakfast or brunch.

Eggs Baked with Havarti

2	tablespoons cream
2	eggs

Season All
Havarti

Decide how many servings needed and follow directions for each serving. Spray ramekin cups with cooking spray. Put cream in each and break eggs in each. Sprinkle with season all and shredded Havarti cheese. Bake at 425 degrees for 18 to 20 minutes until lightly browned and puffed.

Karen Scarborough, Owner/Chef Thyme Away Bed and Breakfast

Quiche of the Day

3 eggs, beaten
1 cup milk
4 ounces shredded Swiss
  cheese
2 tablespoons flour
  Nutmeg

1 tablespoon onion
1 meat of choice
  (ham, bacon, crabmeat, etc.)
1 cup vegetables (spinach,
  mushrooms, broccoli, etc.)
1 unbaked pie shell
  Salt and pepper to taste

Combine everything in a large bowl. Mix well and pour into pie shell. Bake at 350 degrees for 45 minutes or until set.

Shirred Eggs

12 slices bacon
12 eggs
  Milk
  Butter

  Salt
24 saltine crackers
  Paprika

Spray muffin pan with cooking spray. Cook bacon until done but not crisp. Line each muffin cup with a slice of bacon. Put 1 teaspoon bacon drippings in each cup. Put 1 egg in each cup and dot with butter. Add a teaspoon of milk to each. Crumble 2 crackers over each egg and sprinkle with paprika. Bake at 350 for 15 to 18 minutes until tops are browned and bubbly.

Karen Scarborough, Owner/Chef Thyme Away Bed and Breakfast

These can be prepared the night before and baked the following morning. Do allow extra cooking time if they have been refrigerated.

Sausage and Cheese Grits

1	pound sausage		3	tablespoons unsalted butter
1	quart water		1/8	teaspoon garlic powder
3/4	teaspoon salt		1/2	teaspoon Tabasco sauce
1	cup stone ground or quick cooking grits		2	large, lightly beaten eggs
1	cup grated, sharp Cheddar cheese		1-2	green onions, as garnish

Preheat oven to 350 degrees and grease a 2 quart baking dish with butter. Fry sausage until browned. Drain and set aside. Boil water and salt. Add grits. Cook until thickened. Remove from heat and add sausage, cheese, butter and garlic powder and hot sauces. Add eggs, stirring briskly. Spoon into prepared dish. Bake at 350 degrees for 35 to 40 minutes or until puffed and lightly set. Garnish with green onions. Makes 8 servings.

Grits are becoming increasingly popular as a side dish. Try this dish with a steak and side salad.

Gruyère Cheese Grits

1	quart whole milk		1	teaspoon salt
1/2	cup butter, divided		1/2	teaspoon garlic powder
1 1/2	cups shredded Gruyère cheese		1/4	teaspoon freshly ground pepper
1	cup uncooked grits		1/3	cup grated Parmesan cheese

Bring milk to boil in a large, heavy saucepan. Add 1/4 cup butter and Gruyère cheese. Stir until cheese melts. Slowly add grits. Boil until thick, stirring constantly. Stir in seasonings. Reduce heat to low. Beat mixture at low speed with an electric mixer for 5 minutes. Pour into lightly greased 8 x 8 inch square pan. Melt remaining 1/4 cup butter and mix with Parmesan cheese. Spread over top of grits mixture. Bake at 350 degrees for 30 minutes. Makes 8 to 10 servings.

Can be made ahead and refrigerated before cooking.

Sausage Mushroom Breakfast Casserole

2¼ cups seasoned croutons
1½ pounds pork sausage
4 eggs, beaten
2¼ cups whole milk
1 (10¾ ounce) can cream of mushroom soup, undiluted
1 (4 ounce) can sliced mushrooms, drained

¾ teaspoon dry mustard
2 cups shredded Cheddar cheese
 Cherry tomato halves, optional
 Parsley sprigs, optional

Spread croutons in a lightly greased, 9 x 13 inch baking dish and set aside. Cook sausage until browned, stirring to crumble and drain well. Sprinkle over croutons. Combine eggs, milk, soup, mushrooms and mustard, mixing well. Pour over sausage. Cover and refrigerate at least 8 hours, or overnight.

Remove from refrigerator and let stand 30 minutes. Bake, uncovered at 325 degrees for 50 to 55 minutes. Sprinkle cheese over top and bake an additional 5 minutes or until cheese melts. Garnish with tomatoes and parsley if desired.

Sausage Muffins

1	pound hot or mild sausage	1½	cups grated Cheddar cheese
1	small jar Cheese Whiz	1	package English muffins

In a medium-sized frying page, brown sausage and drain. Add Cheese Whiz and Cheddar cheese to the pan and stir until melted and mixed well. Spread mixture onto halved English muffins. Freeze until set. Bake at 350 degrees for 10 to 15 minutes or until browned.

These are great to keep in the freezer. You can take 1 to 2 out as need for an easy and quick breakfast.

Sweet Kugel

1	package medium noodles, cooked and drained	1	(8 ounce) carton sour cream, room temperature
6	eggs	2	sticks butter
2	cups sugar	2	cups cornflakes, crushed
12	ounces cream cheese, room temperature		

Mix noodles with eggs, sugar, cream cheese, and sour cream. Melt butter in 9 x 13 inch baking dish. Reserve some butter to mix with cornflakes. Add noodle mixture to dish. Mix cornflakes with butter to moisten. Sprinkle on top of noodles. Cover with foil and bake at 350 degrees for 1 hour. Uncover and bake 30 minutes longer, checking frequently so top doesn't burn.

Kerri Vice, Owner/Chef Table Toppers Catering Co.

Desserts

FUN

WOMEN TURN PASTIMES INTO PASSIONS

All work and no play was never the prescribed regimen for Southern women. But even when they are having fun, women of the South make big things happen.

Being heralded as the "garden spot of America and paradise of the world" in an 1889 news report, LaGrange earned such praise thanks to the favorite hobby of women of that time: gardening. Mary Jane Bigham turned her gardening into a social affair by hosting parties to coincide with the blooming of her rare flowers. One such party celebrated the arrival of her night blooming cereus, a specimen that blooms only once every seven years.

Sharing a similar passion for gardening, Elizabeth Curtright Sledge and her friend Sarah Ferrell would order plants together and compete to see whose efforts produced the most impressive results. The competition was fierce as both women created gardens of excellence.

The Ferrell Gardens, purchased in 1911 by the Callaway family and renamed Hills and Dales, continued to flourish under the loving and talented care of Ida Cason Callaway and Alice Hand Callaway. Expanding the formal boxwood garden and adding fountains and statuary, the Callaways created a breathtaking paradise that inspired more than a few courting couples from nearby LaGrange College to fall in love.

From courting to the court, another pastime turned passion for the women of LaGrange was basketball. In a time when no sports teams existed for women, Stella Bradfield pioneered fun by coaching LaGrange High School's first female basketball team. With such accomplishments as earning a master's degree in psychology at Columbia University, opening a local school for boys and establishing the education department at LaGrange College, perhaps one of Stella's most satisfying achievements was leading her 1918 basketball team in their undefeated season.

Desserts

Atlanta Coca Cola Cake

CAKE

3	tablespoons cocoa	½	cup small marshmallows
2	cups sugar	1	cup cola
2	cups flour	½	cup buttermilk
½	cup butter	1	teaspoon soda
½	cup oil	1	teaspoon vanilla extract
2	eggs		

ICING

½	cup butter	6	tablespoons cola
3	tablespoons cocoa	1	box powdered sugar
1	tablespoon vanilla extract	1	cup chopped nuts, optional

Prepare cake first by mixing sugar and flour. Bring butter, oil, cocoa, and cola to boil. Pour over dry ingredients and mix well. Add buttermilk, soda, eggs, and vanilla extract; mix well. Fold in marshmallows. Bake in 9 x 13 inch pan for 40 to 50 minutes at 350 degrees.

For the icing, bring the butter, cocoa and cola to a boil. Add the sugar, vanilla extract and nuts. Mix well and spread on cake.

Carrot Pineapple Layer Cake

CAKE

1¼	cups vegetable oil	4	eggs
2	cups sugar	1	(16 ounce) can crushed pineapple, drained
2	cups all-purpose flour	4	cups shredded carrots
1	teaspoon baking soda	1	cup raisins
2	teaspoons baking powder	1	cup chopped pecans, optional
1	teaspoon salt		
2	teaspoons ground cinnamon		

FILLING

1	cup sugar	½	cup butter
2	tablespoons all-purpose flour	1	cup chopped pecans, optional
¼	teaspoon salt	1	teaspoon vanilla extract
1	cup whipping cream		

Preheat oven to 350 degrees. Beat oil and sugar for 1 minute on medium speed, and until creamy. Combine remaining dry ingredients and add to creamed mixture alternating with eggs. Stir in all remaining ingredients and pour into 3 greased 9 inch round pans. Bake for 35 to 40 minutes. Let cool on wire racks.

For filling mix sugar, flour and salt in a medium saucepan. Stir in cream and add butter. Cook, stirring constantly, until butter is melted. Bring to a boil and let simmer for 30 minutes, stirring occasionally. Stir in pecans and vanilla extract. Remove from heat and immediately spread between layers of cake. Can drizzle top with the filling or can top with your favorite cream cheese icing. Serves 10 to 15.

When baking most cakes it's best to use a shiny pan to prevent darkening of the bottom and sides.

Chocolate Cheesecake

CRUST
2 cups graham cracker crumbs
3 tablespoons sugar

4 ounces butter, melted

CAKE
3 (8 ounce) packages cream cheese
1 cup sugar
1½ cups plain yogurt

12 ounces bittersweet chocolate
2½ cups heavy whipping cream
¼ ounce gelatin

For crust, mix graham cracker crumbs and sugar together by hand. Add melted butter. Work mixture together with hands. Place ⅔ of mixture in bottom of a 10 inch springform pan. Press down into bottom using a flat bottom beverage glass. Put the rest of the crumb mixture around the edges of the pan with the glass, using a rolling motion. Bake at 400 degrees for 5 minutes. Remove and cool.

For cake, cream sugar and cream cheese in a blender on medium speed for about 5 minutes. Add yogurt and continue to blend for another 2 minutes. Place in a bowl and set aside. In a blender, whip heavy cream to medium peaks and set aside.

Melt chocolate in a double boiler over medium heat and set aside.

Bloom gelatin in ½ cup cold water. Once it has bloomed, mix in 2 tablespoons of hot water from the bottom of the double boiler and mix back to a liquid consistency.

Add gelatin to melted chocolate and stir until completely blended. Mix this into the cream cheese mixture until completely blended. Gently fold this into the heavy cream. Fold it until just blended. Do not over mix.

Spoon mixture into graham cracker crust. Once filled, place it in the freezer for 3 to 4 hours. Remove cake from freezer and take the springform sides off the pan. Allow cake to come to room temperature, cut and serve. Garnish with chocolate or caramel sauce.

John Bell, Owner/Chef Ou lá lá'

Dirt Cake

1   (20 ounce) package
     chocolate sandwich cookies
1   (8 ounce) cream cheese,
     softened
½   teaspoon butter
1   cup powdered sugar

3½ cups whole or 2% milk
2   packages French vanilla or
     chocolate pudding
1   (12 ounce) extra creamy
     Cool Whip

Crumble cookies in blender until they look like dark brown dirt. Set aside. Cream remainder of the ingredients together in a large bowl. Stir together well. Starting and ending with cookie crumbs, layer the mixtures together in serving dish. Chill overnight. Makes 10 to 12 servings.

Do not make pudding according to package directions as the powder is just used for taste.

4th of July Strawberry Surprise

2   large baskets strawberries,
     divided
2   tablespoons sugar

2   tablespoons white wine
1   vanilla pudding cake
2   tubs Cool Whip

Purée 1 basket of strawberries, sugar and white wine in blender. Set aside. Line bottom of 2½ quart dish with pieces of cake sliced about 1 inch thick. Pour half of strawberry sauce over cake pieces. Slice remaining strawberries and make a single layer of thin sliced strawberries over the cake. Spread 1 tub Cool Whip over cake pieces. Cover mixture with another layer of cake pieces. Repeat previous steps in same order with sauce, strawberries and Cool Whip. Decorate top with strawberries. Use remaining berries for garnish. Serve immediately or chill until ready to serve.

Lemon Cheese Cake from South Georgia or Caramel Cake

(you choose the filling)

The idea behind this recipe is to choose 1 flavor of cake layer and 1 filling flavor. Or just make both for double the treat!

WHITE LAYERED CAKE

6 eggs, separated (you will use whites for the cake and yolks for filling)
2 cups sugar
1 cup butter or shortening
1 cup sweet milk
3½ cups plain flour, sifted
2 teaspoons baking powder

Whip the egg whites to stiff peaks. In a separate bowl, cream together the sugar and butter. Add the milk and flour alternately to the creamed mixture, ending with flour. Gently fold in the egg whites and the baking powder. Divide into 3 (8 inch) pans and bake at 300 degrees until just firm. Don't overcook.

YELLOW LAYERED CAKE

1 cup butter
2 cups sugar
2½-3 cups flour, sifted twice
4 eggs, 1 at a time
2 teaspoons vanilla extract
½ teaspoon baking soda
1 cup buttermilk

Cream butter and sugar well, add eggs and vanilla extract. In a separate bowl, blend flour and baking soda. Add flour mixture to the creamed mixture alternately with the buttermilk, ending with the flour mixture. Divide and bake as white layered cake above.

LEMON CHEESE FILLING

6 egg yolks
1 cup sugar
2 lemons, zested
½ cup lemon juice
1 stick butter

Cream egg yolks and sugar. Add all ingredients to double boiler, stirring constantly. Cook until thick as jelly. Spread on cake layers when cooled.

CARAMEL CAKE FILLING

2 cups sugar	1 teaspoon baking soda
1 cup buttermilk	½ cup butter

Cook all ingredients together in a deep saucepan until it comes to a boil, then turn the heat down some. Continue cooking until it forms a small ball in cold water. Beat well until creamy and spread on the cake layers.

Betty Daniel, Owner/Chef Taste of Lemon

If filling becomes too thick, add some whipping cream to make it spread a little easier.

German Bundt Cinnamon Cake

CAKE

1 box yellow cake mix	1 teaspoon butter flavoring
1 small box vanilla instant pudding	4 eggs
	1 cup chopped nuts, divided
¾ cup vegetable oil	¼ cup sugar
¾ cup water	2 teaspoons vanilla extract
1 teaspoon vanilla extract	2 teaspoons cinnamon

GLAZE

1 cup powdered sugar	½ teaspoon vanilla extract
3 tablespoons milk	½ teaspoon butter flavoring

Stir together the cake mix and instant pudding mix. Add oil, water, vanilla extract and butter flavoring. Mix well. Add eggs 1 at a time. Beat mixture very well for 8 minutes. Grease a Bundt cake pan heavily. Sprinkle ¼ cup of the nuts in the bottom of the pan. Combine remaining nuts, sugar and cinnamon. Layer cake batter in pan alternating with sugar mixture. Bake for 45 minutes at 325 degrees.

Mix all ingredients together for glaze and drizzle on top of cooled cake.

8 Pound Strawberry Cake

According to this chef, if you make 1½ recipes of this cake and with enough strawberries, purée and brandy, you will have an 8 Pound Strawberry Cake! It is so yummy!

CAKE

2⅓ cups plain flour
2½ teaspoons baking powder
½ teaspoon salt
1 small package strawberry flavored gelatin
2 cups sugar

1 cup butter, softened
4 large eggs
1 cup milk
1 teaspoon vanilla extract
½ cup strawberry purée

FILLING

1½ cups heavy whipping cream
2 tablespoons sugar
½ teaspoon powdered sugar
½ teaspoon vanilla extract

1-2 pounds fresh strawberries, sliced
1 cup strawberry purée
¼ cup brandy

FROSTING

1½ cups butter, softened
1 (8 ounce) package cream cheese, room temperature

4 cups powdered sugar, sifted
2 teaspoons vanilla and or strawberry flavoring

Preheat oven to 350 degrees and grease and flour 2 (8 inch) cake pans. Mix flour, baking powder, salt and dry gelatin in small bowl. In a separate bowl, beat together sugar and butter until creamy. Add the eggs to the creamed mixture one at a time. Once incorporated, add the vanilla, scraping the sides. Add the strawberry purée. Pour batter into buttered and floured pans (or use floured cooking spray) and bake for 25 to 30 minutes or until done. Cool 10 minutes and remove from pans to wire rack to cool completely. Torte each layer into 2 layers, this will yield 4 total layers.

Chill a metal bowl for beating cream. Beat heavy whipping cream, sugars, and vanilla extract until stiff. Place 1 cake layer on plate and saturate or brush the top of each layer with the strawberry purée and brandy. Spread whipped cream mixture on top and completely cover with fresh strawberry slices. Top with second layer and continue with layers. Do not place purée or cream on top, as this will be frosted.

For the frosting, beat butter and cream cheese on low speed until blended well. Mix in powdered sugar and vanilla until creamy. Frost the sides and top of the cake. Top the cake with sliced or whole strawberries for garnish. Store in refrigerator.

Kerri Vice, Owner/Chef Table Toppers Catering Co

Jello Cake

1 box white cake mix	1 (8 ounce) carton Cool Whip
1 box orange Jello	1 can Mandarin oranges

Prepare cake as directed on back of box. After cake cooks, poke holes in cake with toothpick. Prepare Jello as directed on back of box. Pour Jello mixture all over cake. Refrigerate until Jello sets, then smooth Cool Whip on top. Place Mandarin oranges on top as garnish.

Lemon Dream Cake

CAKE

1 box lemon cake mix	1 cup apricot nectar
½ cup sugar	4 eggs
½ cup oil	

ICING

1 stick butter	1 cup sour cream
2 cups sugar	1 teaspoon grated lemon rind
2 tablespoons cornstarch	Juice of 1 lemon

For cake, place all ingredients in medium-sized bowl and beat for 4 minutes. Pour equal amounts into 4 well-greased and floured round cake pans. Bake at 300 degrees for about 30 minutes, or until done.

For icing, place all ingredients in saucepan and bring to a boil. Cook for 1 minute after boiling begins. Put icing on layers of cake one at a time to let it soak in.

Mint Chocolate Chip Cheesecake

CRUST

2   **cups finely crushed chocolate wafers (about 36-38 cookies)**

½   **cup butter (no substitutes), melted**

FILLING

2   **(8 ounce) packages cream cheese, softened**

1   **cup sugar**

⅓   **cup green crème de menthe liqueur**

3   **eggs**

3   **(8 ounce) cartons sour cream**

1   **cup miniature semisweet chocolate pieces**

TOPPING

1   **ounce block semisweet chocolate**

1   **teaspoon shortening**

Combine crushed wafers and butter in a medium mixing bowl; toss gently. Press mixture on bottom and 2 inches up sides of a 9 inch springform pan. Set aside.

For filling, beat cream cheese and sugar in a large mixing bowl, using an electric mixer, until smooth. Beat in crème de menthe. Add eggs all at once, beating on slow speed just until combined. Stir in sour cream until combined and stir in the semisweet chocolate pieces. Pour filling into crust-lined pan. Set the pan in a shallow baking pan on the oven rack. Bake in a 375 degree oven for 50 to 55 minutes or until the center appears nearly set when shaken. Remove from oven and take springform pan out of baking pan. Leaving the cheesecake in the springform pane, cool on a wire rack for 15 minutes. Use a small metal spatula to loosen crust from sides of pan. Cool 30 minutes or more. Remove sides of pan. Cool 1 hour; cover and chill at least 4 hours.

For topping, melt chocolate and shortening in a small saucepan over low heat. Drizzle melted chocolate over the top of the chilled cheesecake. Chill until set.

White Chocolate Raspberry Cheesecake

CRUST
1⅓ **cups graham cracker crumbs**	1 **tablespoon butter**
¼ **cup sugar**	3 **cups fresh raspberries**

FILLING
3 **(8 ounce) packages cream cheese**	2 **teaspoons vanilla extract**
1 **cup sugar**	¼ **teaspoon salt**
¼ **cup Amaretto**	3 **ounces white chocolate, melted**
2 **tablespoons flour**	3 **large eggs**

Combine first 3 ingredients of crust. Press firmly into the bottom of a springform pan and up 1 inch of the sides. Wrap outside of pan with tin foil. Arrange berries over crust and set aside.

For filling, place cream cheese in a large bowl and beat on medium speed until smooth. Add sugar and next 5 ingredients and beat until smooth. Add eggs one at a time, beating well after each. Pour filling into springform pan. Place in large shallow baking pan and add hot water around the cheesecake to a depth of 1 inch. Bake for 1 hour and 10 minutes at 325 degrees. Remove from oven and cool to room temperature. Cover and chill at least 4 hours. Serves 12.

New York Cheesecake

CRUST

1¾ cups vanilla wafers	½ cup butter, melted

FILLING

4 (8 ounce) packages cream cheese	5 eggs
1 cup sugar	⅓ cup cream
3 tablespoons flour	1 teaspoon vanilla extract

TOPPING

1 cup sour cream	½ teaspoon vanilla extract
2 tablespoons sugar	

Mix crust ingredients and press into bottom of a springform pan. For filling, mix cheese, sugar and flour until smooth. Add eggs slowly. Add cream and vanilla extract. Bake at 350 degrees for 15 minutes, and then at 200 degrees for 1 hour 20 minutes. Mix the topping ingredients and pour over cake. Bake 15 more minutes at 200 degrees.

Jamie Keating, Owner/Chef Gourmet Events

An easy way to crush Oreos is to put them in a zip-top baggie and pound them.

Buster Bar Dessert

1 (1 pound) bag Oreo cookies	2 (16 ounce) jars hot fudge ice cream sauce
¾ stick butter, melted	
½ gallon vanilla ice cream	1 (16 ounce) carton Cool Whip, unfrozen and softened
1 (12½ ounce) can redskin peanuts	

Crush Oreos. Pour butter over Oreos. Mix well. Pack into the bottom of a 13 x 8 inch baking dish. Freeze until hardened (about 30 minutes). Soften ice cream and spread over Oreos. Sprinkle redskin peanuts over ice cream. Warm hot fudge until hot and spreadable. Spoon over nuts. Top with Cool Whip. Keep in freezer until ready to serve. Makes 8 to 10 servings.

Old-Fashioned Chocolate Sheet Cake

CAKE

2 cups all-purpose flour	3 heaping tablespoons cocoa
2 cups sugar	1 teaspoon baking soda
½ teaspoon salt	½ cup buttermilk
1 stick butter	2 eggs, slightly beaten
1 cup water	1 teaspoon vanilla extract
½ cup vegetable oil	

ICING

1 stick butter	6 tablespoons milk
3 heaping tablespoons cocoa	1 box powdered sugar, sifted

Preheat oven to 350 degrees. In a large bowl mix flour, sugar, salt. Set aside. In a saucepan put 1 stick of butter, water, oil and cocoa. Mix then bring to a boil, remove from heat. In another bowl mix backing soda and buttermilk together then add eggs and vanilla extract. Mix everything together and pour into a greased cookie sheet with sides. Bake 20 to 25 minutes. To make icing, melt butter, cocoa and milk together in a saucepan but do not boil. Take off heat and add powdered sugar. Spread over cake immediately.

1 cup of chopped pecans may be added to the icing just before it is spread on cake.

Piña Colada Cake

1 (18½ ounce) box white cake mix with pudding
1 (14 ounce) can sweetened condensed milk
1 (8 ounce) can cream of coconut
1 (20 ounce) can crushed pineapple, drained
1 (16 ounce) carton Cool Whip, thawed
1 (6 ounce) package coconut Chopped pecans and cherries, optional

Mix cake mix and spread in 9 x 13 inch dish. Bake according to directions on cake mix. While baking, combine milk, coconut and pineapples. Make small holes in warm, cooked cake and pour mixture on top. Frost with Cool Whip and coconut once cooled. Top with pecans and cherries for garnish.

Pineapple Orange Sunshine Cake

CAKE
1 box yellow cake mix
½ cup vegetable oil
4 eggs
1 (11 ounce) can Mandarin oranges, undrained

FROSTING
1 (20 ounce) can crushed pineapple, undrained
1 tablespoon sugar
1 (10 ounce) package cheesecake filling mix
1 (8 ounce) carton sour cream
1 (9 ounce) carton Cool Whip

Combined cake mix, oil, eggs, oranges. Mix at medium speed 1 to 2 minutes or until almost smooth. Spoon into 3 greased and floured round cake pans. Bake at 325 degrees for 15 to 20 minutes or until done. Cool cakes in pans for 10 minutes, remove from pans and cool completely on a wire rack. For frosting, combine pineapple, sugar, cheesecake mix and sour cream. Stir until mixture thickens. Fold in Cool Whip, mixing thoroughly. Spread frosting on top, sides and between all layers of cake. Store in refrigerator.

Velvet Voodoo Cake

1	package Duncan Hines devil's food cake mix
1	(3¾ ounce) package instant chocolate pudding
1	cup sour cream
½	cup vegetable oil

½	cup prepared coffee
½	cup dark rum
4	eggs
2	cups semisweet chocolate chips
	Powdered sugar

Combine all ingredients except chocolate chips in a mixing bowl. Mix on low speed just to blend ingredients. Beat at medium speed for 1 minute. Scrape sides of bowl and beat 1 minute more. Fold in chocolate chips. Pour into well greased and floured Bundt pan. Bake at 300 degrees for 70 minutes. Check for doneness — when a toothpick comes out clean it is ready. Cool in pan for 30 minutes. Turn out on to platter and dust with powdered sugar.

Toothpick may come out with chocolate on it from the chocolate chips even though the cake may be done so be careful!

Cherry Nut Crunch

1	large can crushed pineapple
1	large can cherry pie filling
1	box yellow cake mix

1	stick butter
1	cup chopped pecans
¼	cup sugar

Preheat oven to 350 degrees. Lightly grease a 9 x 13 inch baking dish. Place pineapple (do not drain) and pie filling in dish and sprinkle with dry cake mix. Melt butter and pour over cake mix. Sprinkle pecans and sugar on top. Bake for 20 minutes and remove from oven. With a spoon, poke holes through the mixture to allow juices to seep through. Bake for 20 to 25 minutes longer.

This is an excellent cake to serve to guests you want to impress. Try serving it with whipped cream, ice cream or fresh strawberry accents.

Ice Cream Delight

1   (12 count) package ice cream sandwiches
1   (7 ounce) bag malted milk balls
1   (8 ounce) carton Cool Whip
1   small bottle chocolate syrup

Line the bottom of a 9 x 13 inch casserole dish with ice cream sandwiches. Chop malt balls and reserve some for garnish. Mix the rest with the Cool Whip. Spread Cool Whip mixture on top of ice cream sandwiches. Pour stripes of syrup on top of dish and sprinkle more bits of crushed malt balls.

Try substituting malt balls with crushed Butterfinger, Heath, or Oreos for a different taste!

Chocolate Éclair Pie

2   small packages French vanilla pudding
3½ cups cold milk, divided
1   (12 ounce) tub Cool Whip
1   box graham crackers
½   stick butter
⅓   cup cocoa
⅛   teaspoon salt
1   cup sugar
1   teaspoon vanilla extract

Combine pudding packages with milk and stir well, until it starts to thicken. Add in Cool Whip. Line a 9 x 13 inch pan with graham crackers. Pour half of filling in pan and smooth out. Line pan with more crackers and add remaining filling. Finish with more graham crackers. Refrigerate.

In a small saucepan, combine butter, milk, cocoa, salt and sugar. Bring to a boil for 1 minute, stirring completely. Remove from heat, add vanilla extract. Cool completely and pour on top of mixture. Cool for a day or overnight.

Almond Pumpkin Pie

CRUST
⅓ cup all-purpose flour	½ cup shortening
½ teaspoon salt	3 tablespoons cold water

ALMOND LAYER
1 cup finely chopped almonds	3 tablespoons butter, softened
½ cup firmly packed brown sugar	2 teaspoons all-purpose flour
	¼ teaspoon almond extract

PUMPKIN FILLING
1¼ cups granulated brown sugar	1 tablespoon molasses
3 ounces cream cheese, softened	1 teaspoon cinnamon
2 eggs	½ teaspoon nutmeg
1¼ cups canned solid pack pumpkin	½ teaspoon salt
½ cup evaporated milk	¼ teaspoon ginger
⅓ cup sour cream	⅛ teaspoon ground clove
	½ teaspoon almond extract

For crust spoon flour into measuring cup and level. Combine flour and salt in medium bowl. Cut in Crisco using two knives until all flour is blended to form pea-size chunks. Sprinkle with water, 1 tablespoon at a time. Toss lightly with fork until dough will form a ball. Press dough between hands to form 5 to 6 inch pancake. Flour lightly on both sides. Roll between sheets of waxed paper on dampened countertop until 1 inch larger than upside down 9 inch pie plate. Peel off of sheet. Flip into pie plate. Remove other sheet. Fold dough edge under and flute.

For almond layer, combine nuts, brown sugar, butter, flour and almond extract. Toss with fork until well blended. Spoon onto unbaked pie crust. Press firmly onto the bottom and part of the way up the sides. Refrigerate.

For filling combine granulated brown sugar and cream cheese in large bowl. Beat at medium speed of electric mixer until well blended. Beat in eggs, pumpkin, evaporated milk, sour cream and molasses at low speed. Add cinnamon, nutmeg, salt, ginger, cloves and ½ teaspoon almond extract. Beat 1 minute. Spoon over almond layer. Bake at 425 degrees for 15 minutes. Reduce oven temperature to 350 degrees. Bake for 50 to 60 minutes. Cover edge of pie with foil, if needed, to prevent overburning. Cool to room temperature.

Angel Pecan Chocolate Mousse Pie

CRUST

3 egg whites	1 cup crisp round Ritz cracker crumbs
1 cup plus 2 tablespoons sugar	1½ cups chopped pecans
2 teaspoons vanilla extract	

FILLING

4 ounces semisweet good quality chocolate	¼ cup sugar
⅛ cup heavy cream	2 egg whites
¼ cup rum	2 cups heavy cream

Beat egg whites until foamy and stiff. Add 1 cup plus 2 tablespoons sugar, a little at a time, beating after each addition. Add 1 teaspoon of vanilla extract and continue beating until mixture holds soft. Mix cracker crumbs and 1 cup of pecans then fold into the meringue mixture, a little at a time. Spoon entire mixture into an 8 inch pie plate to form a shell. Pull up mixture into peaks around the edge of the pie plate, leaving room for a filling. Bake at 350 for 30 minutes. Cool thoroughly on wire cake rack.

For the filling, place chocolate in double boiler over hot water. Melt chocolate slowly and stir in heavy cream. Let cool to room temperature. In another saucepan, heat slowly and dissolve sugar and rum. Add to chocolate mixture. While chocolate mixture cools, whip heavy cream until stiff and set aside. In separate bowl beat egg whites until fluffy and stiff. When chocolate mixture has cooled fold in egg whites and then fold in whipped cream. Mousse filling is best if made 8 hours before serving and must sit a minimum of 3 hours before serving. Once shell has cooled and mousse is set, add filling to shell. Filling can set up in the shell of the pie or a separate bowl. Serves 8 to 10 people.

Cream Cheese Pie

PIE

1	(8 ounce) package cream cheese	½	teaspoon vanilla extract
½	cup sugar	1	dash salt
1	tablespoon lemon juice	2	eggs
		1	graham cracker pie shell

TOPPING

1	cup sour cream	¼	teaspoon vanilla extract
2	tablespoons sugar		Fresh fruit of choice

Mix all of pie ingredients together and pour in graham cracker pie shell. Bake at 325 degrees for 25 to 30 minutes. Cool for at least 15 minutes. Mix together all topping ingredients. Add topping to the pie and chill well. Top with fresh fruit and serve.

Fudge Pie

3	tablespoons cocoa	2	eggs, slightly beaten
1	teaspoon flour	½	cup evaporated milk or cream
1¼	cups sugar	1	teaspoon vanilla extract
½	stick butter, melted and slightly cooled	1	unbaked pie shell

Mix cocoa, flour and sugar together. In a separate bowl, blend the melted butter, eggs, evaporated milk and vanilla extract. Mix dry ingredients and liquid ingredients. Pour into unbaked pie shell and bake at 350 degrees for about 45 minutes, or until firm. If the crust starts to brown too quickly, cover with foil around the edges.

Betty Daniel, Owner/Chef Taste of Lemon

When serving, add a topping of ice cream or whipped cream with a little Kahlúa or Amaretto to taste. Also, toasted walnuts or pecans add that little special touch.

Fresh Georgia Peach Pie

1   (8 ounce) package cream
     cheese
1   cup powdered sugar
1   graham cracker crust

4-6 slices of fresh peaches
1   (8 ounce) carton of Cool
     Whip
     Mint sprig, optional

With mixer, beat cream cheese with powdered sugar until smooth. Spread over graham cracker crust. Place fresh sliced peaches on top of cream cheese mixture. Top with Cool Whip. Garnish with a slice of fresh peach and mint sprig.

Can substitute Dream Whip for Cool Whip.

Gooey Georgian Pie

1   (8 ounce) package cream
     cheese
1   cup powdered sugar
1   cup crunchy peanut butter
¼   cup milk
1   (8 ounce) carton Cool Whip,
     divided

1   deep dish baked pie crust
¼   cup peanut butter or
     chocolate chip morsels,
     optional
     Chocolate syrup, optional

Mix all ingredients, reserving ¼ of Cool Whip for topping. Pour mixture into pie crust and chill several hours. Top with remaining Cool Whip. Sprinkle morsels on top and drizzle chocolate syrup on top of pie.

Several variations can be made to this recipe. A large graham cracker or Oreo crust can be substituted for the pie crust. Using smooth peanut butter instead of crunchy gives it a different texture. Also try sprinkling crushed peanuts on the top of the pie.

Grits Pie

1	cup stone ground grits cooked and cooled slightly	2	tablespoons butter, melted
1	cup brown sugar	1	teaspoon vanilla extract
2	teaspoons plain flour	1	teaspoon white vinegar
2	large eggs, lightly beaten	1	(9 inch) unbaked, regular size pie shell
4	tablespoons whole milk		

Preheat the oven to 350 degrees. In a bowl, combine the grits, brown sugar, flour, and eggs. Blend well, then stir in milk and butter. Add the vanilla extract and vinegar, and blend well. Pour the mixture into the pie shell and bake for 35 to 40 minutes, or until the center is just set. Let cool briefly, then serve while still warm. Serve warm.

Kerri Vice, Owner/Chef Table Toppers Catering Co.

This is excellent alone, but is also great with vanilla ice cream or freshly whipped cream.

Kentucky Pie

PIE

1	cup chopped pecans Bourbon	½	cup butter, melted
1	cup sugar	6	ounces semisweet chocolate chips
6	tablespoons flour	1½	teaspoons vanilla extract
2	eggs	1	(9 inch) unbaked pie shell

CREAM MIXTURE

1	cup cream, whipped	1	teaspoon vanilla extract
3	tablespoons sugar		

Soak pecans with bourbon in small bowl overnight. Drain pecans. Preheat oven to 325 degrees. Combine sugar and flour and add remaining pie ingredients. Pour into unbaked pie shell. Bake for 50 to 60 minutes. Combine all ingredients to make the cream mixture. Serve pie with cream mixture spread on top.

The best grits to use are, of course, Speckled Heart Stone-Ground Grits from Callaway Gardens in Pine Mountain, Georgia

Hershey Bar Pie

7   **Hershey Almond Bars**   1   **graham cracker crust**
1   **(12 ounce) carton Cool Whip**

Break up Hershey Almond Bars and place in microwave for 1 minute on high. Let stand 15 to 20 seconds. Mix with Cool Whip. Pour into graham cracker crust and freeze.

Japanese Fruit Pie

½   **cup butter**   ½   **cup raisins**
1   **cup sugar**   ½   **cup coconut**
1   **teaspoon vanilla extract**   ½   **cup pecans**
1   **tablespoon vinegar**   1   **(9 inch) unbaked pie crust**
2   **eggs, beaten**

Preheat oven to 350 degrees. Slowly mix butter, sugar, vanilla extract, vinegar and eggs. Mix until smooth. Then fold in the raisins, coconut, and pecans. Pour into pie shell. Bake for 45 to 50 minutes. Serve slightly warm.

Macaroon Pie

3   **egg whites**   12   **saltine crackers, finely**
¼   **teaspoon baking powder**   **crushed**
1   **cup sugar**   12   **dates chopped fine**
1   **teaspoon almond extract**   **(or ⅓ pound chopped dates)**
                                           ½   **cup chopped pecans**

Beat egg whites until stiff. Slowly add baking powder, sugar and extract. Fold in remaining ingredients. Pour into 9 inch pie pan. Bake 30 minutes at 350 degrees. Serve with fresh whipped cream. Makes 8 servings.

New Orleans Pecan Pie

2	eggs, separated	¼	teaspoon salt
1	cup sour cream	1	(9 inch) pie crust, baked
1	cup sugar	1	cup brown sugar
¼	cup flour	1	cup chopped pecans
½	teaspoon vanilla extract		

In a saucepan, combine egg yolks and next 5 ingredients. Cook over medium heat, stirring until thickened. Pour into baked pie shell. In large bowl, beat egg whites until soft peaks form. Gradually add brown sugar and continue beating until stiff. While filling is still warm, spread egg white mixture over it. Sprinkle with pecans. Bake at 375 degrees for 12 to 15 minutes or until golden brown. Serves 8.

Old-Fashioned Buttermilk Pie

1½	cups sugar	1	stick melted butter (real butter is best)
2	tablespoons (heaping) self-rising flour	1	teaspoon vanilla extract
¼	cup buttermilk	1	(9 inch) frozen deep dish pie crust
3	eggs		

Combine ingredients in the order they are listed and mix well. Pour in pie crust. Bake at 350 degrees for 50 minutes. Cool for 1 to 2 hours to let pie set.

You can enjoy this pie straight out of the oven, but you may need to use a spoon!

Peanut Butter Pie

CRUST

1	cup graham cracker crumbs	2	tablespoons sugar
3	tablespoons butter, melted	2	tablespoons cocoa

FILLING

12	ounces cream cheese, softened	1½	teaspoons vanilla extract
1½	cups peanut butter	1½	cups whipping cream
1½	cups sugar	¾	cup milk chocolate chips

Preheat oven to 325 degrees. To make crust combine graham cracker crumbs, butter, sugar and cocoa in a bowl. Press into the bottom of a 10 inch round springform pan. Bake for 10 minutes. Remove from oven and cool.

To make filling: in a large bowl combine cream cheese, peanut butter, sugar and vanilla extract. Beat on medium speed until smooth. In separate bowl, beat whipping cream until soft peaks form. Fold into peanut butter mixture. Spoon mixture into cooled crust. Sprinkle chocolate chips over pie.

Southern Strawberry Pie

1	cup sugar	4	cups fresh strawberries, halved
1	cup water	1	(9 inch) pastry shell, baked
3	tablespoons cornstarch		Cool Whip
¼	cup strawberry Jello, unmade		

Bring the first 3 ingredients to a boil in saucepan over medium heat. Stir constantly for 1 minute or until thickened. Stir in Jello powder until dissolved. Remove from heat and chill 1 hour. Arrange strawberries in pastry shell and pour gelatin mixture over strawberries. Cover and chill 2 hours. Uncover and top with Cool Whip.

Apple Dumplin's

1   (8 count) can crescent rolls
    Cinnamon sugar
2   Granny Smith apples, peeled,
    cored and cut in fourths

1   stick butter
¾   cup sugar
1   cup orange juice

Separate crescent rolls into 8 triangles. Sprinkle each crescent triangle with sugar and roll 1 apple piece into each crescent roll triangle. Place in 9 x 13 inch baking pan. Melt butter and mix in orange juice and sugar. Pour over apples and bake at 325 degrees for 30 minutes. Serves 8.

Apricot Salad

BOTTOM LAYER

2   small packages apricot
    gelatin
1   can crushed pineapple
2   cups cold water

2   cups boiling water
2   large bananas, cubed
1   cup miniature marshmallows

FIRST TOPPING

¾   cup orange juice
1   tablespoon butter
¾   cup sugar

1   egg (slightly beaten)
1   tablespoon cornstarch

SECOND TOPPING

1   large package Dream Whip

1   (8 ounce) package cream
    cheese

THIRD TOPPING

1   cup chopped pecans

Mix together all of the bottom layer ingredients and refrigerate to congeal in oblong casserole dish. In a pot on the stove on low heat, stir together all ingredients for first topping. Spread first topping on top of the congealed gelatin. For second topping, prepare the Dream Whip according to the package directions and stir in cream cheese. Spread second topping on top of the first topping. Sprinkle the chopped pecans on top.

Old-Fashioned Banana Pudding

PUDDING (CUSTARD)

- 1¼ cups sugar
- 3 tablespoons cornstarch
- 3 egg yolks (save egg whites)
- 1 (12 ounce) can evaporated milk
- 1½ cups skim or 1% milk
- 1 teaspoon vanilla extract
- 3-4 medium ripe bananas, sliced
- 1 box vanilla wafers

MERINGUE

- Dash salt
- 3 egg whites
- 2-3 drops honey
- ¼ cup sugar

Preheat oven to 350 degrees. To make the custard mix sugar, cornstarch and egg yolks lightly in a medium sized boiler. Gradually add milks. Cook on medium heat, stirring constantly, for 20 minutes or until thick custard consistency forms. Add vanilla extract as mixture begins to thicken. Remove from heat. In a medium sized baking dish, place a layer of vanilla wafers followed by a layer of bananas. Add a layer of custard and repeat, ending with a layer of custard.

To make meringue, add a dash of salt and honey to egg whites. Mix on high speed, in deep bowl, until frothy and thick white. Add sugar and beat on high until thick and fluffy. Spread over last layer of custard. Bake for 10 to 15 minutes or until meringue is light brown. Serves 6 to 8.

Can substitute whole milk for evaporated milk and ¼ cup flour for the cornstarch.

Persimmon Pudding

2	cups persimmon pulp	1	teaspoon cinnamon
2	cups sugar	1	teaspoon ground cloves
2	eggs, well beaten	1	teaspoon nutmeg
2	cups buttermilk	3	cups all-purpose flour
1	teaspoon baking soda	½	cup vegetable oil
1	teaspoon salt		Whipped cream

Preheat oven to 325 degrees. Mix all ingredients in order given in a large bowl. Pour into greased, 9 x 13 inch baking dish. Bake for 1 hour and 15 minutes. Serve with real whipped cream. Makes 12 servings.

True "cooks" will know that this recipe can only be made in the fall when persimmons are in season!

Bourbon Brownies

3	eggs	1	tablespoon bourbon
1¾	cups sugar	1	cup chocolate chips
1	cup butter	1½	cups chopped walnuts
4	heaping tablespoons cocoa		Vanilla ice cream
1½	cups self-rising flour		

Blend eggs and sugar. Melt butter and add cocoa. Add butter mixture to sugar and eggs. Add flour, blending well. Add bourbon, chips and nuts. Mix well. Pour into greased and floured 9 x 13 inch baking pan. Bake at 325 degrees for 25 to 30 minutes or until toothpick inserted in center comes out clean. Serve with vanilla ice cream or caramel sauce.

Vanilla extract can be substituted for bourbon.

Caramel sauce tastes just as well with these brownies as ice cream!

Baklava

Making Baklava at least 24 hours ahead of time is best as the longer it sits, the better it gets.

3½ cups sugar, divided
2½ cups water
2   tablespoons honey
2   teaspoons fresh lemon juice
4   tablespoons ground
    cinnamon, divided

1   pound walnuts or pecans,
    finely chopped
1   pound phyllo pastry dough
1   pound (4 sticks) melted
    butter

In a saucepan, combine 3 cups of sugar, water, honey, lemon juice and 2 tablespoons of ground cinnamon. Bring to a boil, reduce heat and simmer 15 minutes. Take off heat and cool. In a bowl, combine pecans, ½ cup sugar, and 2 tablespoons cinnamon. Unroll thawed phyllo dough on a flat surface. Keep it covered with a damp towel so that sheets don't dry out. Set aside 8 sheets covered while preparing the rest of the dough. Using a pastry brush, brush the bottom of a 15½ x 11½ x 3 inch pan with melted butter. Layer 8 sheets brushing each sheet with butter. Then sprinkle a handful of nut mixture over the dough. Layer 2 more sheets, brushing each with butter. Then sprinkle more nut mixture. Repeat this process until all of the sheets and nut mixture have been used. Layer the last 8 sheets on top. Cut the pastry into diamonds. Pour any remaining butter over pastry. Bake at 300 degrees for 1 to 1½ hours. Pour cooled syrup over hot pastry. Let cool and serve. Makes 50 diamonds.

Cookies In a Cloud

COOKIE

⅓ cup butter, melted	1 cup finely chopped pecans
1 cup firmly packed light brown sugar	2 tablespoons all-purpose flour
	1 tablespoon vanilla extract

CLOUD (WHITE CHOCOLATE MOUSSE)

4 ounces white chocolate	2 cups whipping cream, divided

TOPPING

1 cup purchased caramel sauce	½ cup toasted chopped pecans

For the cookies, stir together butter, brown sugar, pecans, flour and vanilla extract. Drop by heaping teaspoonfuls (use measuring spoon), 5 inches apart, onto aluminum foil lined 9 x 13 pan. Bake at 350 degrees for 8 minutes or until golden brown. Cool on foil, then lift foil and pull from the back of the cookies. Cookies may be made a day or two ahead and kept in an airtight container.

For the White Chocolate Mousse, microwave white chocolate and 1 cup of whipping cream on medium power 3½ minutes or until chocolate melts. Chill, stirring occasionally, until mixture is consistency of soft whipped cream. Beat mixture at low speed with an electric mixer, gradually adding remaining whipping cream. Beat at high speed until stiff peaks form. Do not over beat.

Just before serving, dollop about 3 tablespoons white chocolate mousse on each of twelve cookies. Repeat layers once. Top with a third cookie and remaining mousse (a small dollop). Drizzle with caramel sauce and sprinkle with toasted pecans.

Cream Cheese Bars

CRUST
1	box cake mix with pudding	1	stick butter
1	egg		

TOPPING
2	eggs	1	(8 ounce) package cream
¼	cup all-purpose flour		cheese
1	box powdered sugar		

To make the crust, mix the cake mix, egg and butter in a bowl until mealy. Press flat in a 9 x 13 inch pan. For the topping, combine eggs, flour, and powdered sugar in a small bowl and mix well. Pinch cream cheese off and drop slowly into mixture. Beat until mixed well. Pour over crust and bake at 300 degrees for 30 to 35 minutes.

Éclairs

Éclairs are typically used as a breakfast dish as well as dessert.

½	cup butter	1	(5 ounce) package instant
1	cup water		vanilla pudding mix
1	cup all-purpose flour	1½	cups milk
¼	teaspoon salt	2	cups Cool Whip
4	eggs	1	(16 ounce) container chocolate frosting

Preheat oven to 400 degrees. In a small pan bring butter and water to boil. Add flour and salt, stirring continually until a ball is formed. Remove from heat. Add 1 egg at a time, beating with hand-held mixer until smooth after each egg is added. Spoon on to greased baking sheet. Bake for 20 minutes, or until golden brown. Split each lengthwise, scoop out center and cool each on wire rack. Prepare pudding mix with milk. Blend whipped topping with pudding.

To prepare frosting, place about ⅓ of container into microwavable dish and warm for 20 seconds (just until chocolate is melted). Do not use overcooked chocolate. Drizzle chocolate frosting onto each éclair. Makes 12 servings.

Cream Wafers

WAFERS

1 **cup butter, softened**
⅓ **cup whipping cream**

2 **cups all-purpose flour**
   Sugar

CREAMY FILLING

¾ **cup powdered sugar**
¼ **cup butter, softened**

1 **teaspoon vanilla extract**
   Food coloring, optional

For the wafers, mix thoroughly the butter, cream and flour. Cover and chill for 1 hour, until dough is firm. Preheat oven to 375 degrees. Roll ⅓ of the dough at a time to ⅛ inch thick on a floured surface. Keep remaining dough refrigerated. Cut into 1½ inch circles. Gently transfer each round to foil heavily coated with sugar. Flip so each side is coated. Place on ungreased cookie sheet, and then prick 3 times with a fork. Bake 7 to 9 minutes or just until set, but not brown. Remove from cookie sheet and allow to cool completely.

Prepare filling by creaming all ingredients together, adding food coloring if desired. Spread filling in between wafers to make sandwich.

These are excellent to serve at baby or wedding showers.

Hazelnut Petit Fours

CAKE

2   cups sugar
8   ounces butter
5   eggs, lightly beaten

1½ cups all-purpose flour
¾   cup hazelnut flour

GLAZE

1½ cups water
3   cups sugar
¼   teaspoon cream of tartar

2½ cups powdered sugar
Food coloring
Choice of extract flavoring

For cake, cream sugar and butter in blender on medium speed until light and fluffy. Add eggs in 3 additions, beating thoroughly after each addition. Add flours and blend thoroughly. Pour even amounts of mixture in 3 (9 x 12 inch) greased baking pans. Bake at 325 degrees for 25 to 30 minutes or until toothpick inserted comes out clean. Cool and cut into 1 inch square cubes.

For glaze, mix all ingredients except powdered sugar in heavy bottom pan and boil to 226 degrees. Remove from heat and allow to cool to 110 degrees.

Mix powdered sugar into cooled glaze syrup and add color and flavoring. Dip cakes into mixture 1 at a time. Place on mesh cooling rack and allow to cool for 15 to 20 minutes. Dip cakes again, making sure to get an even coating. Once cooled, feel free to garnish as desired.

John Bell, Chef/Owner Ou lá lá

Lemon Delights

MERINGUES

4	egg whites	1	cup sugar
¼	teaspoon cream of tartar		

FILLING

4	egg yolks	¼	cup bottled lemon juice
½	cup sugar	1	(4½ ounce) carton Cool Whip

Add cream of tartar to egg whites and beat at high speed until soft and forms. Gradually add sugar, beating until stiff. Spoon 1 teaspoonful onto a foil-lined cookie sheet. Make an indention in each spoonful with the spoon for the filling. Bake at 250 degrees for 25 to 30 minutes. Turn oven off and allow meringues to dry thoroughly in the oven. Store in a closed container.

For filling, beat egg yolks, gradually adding sugar. Beat until sugar is dissolved. Blend in lemon juice. Cook in small saucepan in double boiler over medium-low heat stirring constantly until mixture is thick. Remove from heat and store in a covered container in refrigerator (good for 2 days). Just before serving, beat the filling until fluffy and blend in the Cool Whip. Fill each shell with a teaspoon of filling. Yields approximately 35 shells.

Meringue does not set firm if the weather is rainy or damp.

Luscious Lemon Bars

CRUST

½ **cup butter**	1 **cup flour**
¼ **cup powered sugar**	

FILLING

2 **eggs, slightly beaten**	1 **cup sugar**
2 **tablespoons lemon juice and**	2 **tablespoons flour**
a bit of grated rind	**Powdered sugar**
½ **teaspoon baking powder**	

Combine butter, powered sugar and flour for crust. Cut with a pastry blender until it forms a fine even crumbly consistence. Put into a 9 inch square pan. Press on the bottom of the pan until flat and even all over. Bake at 350 degrees for 15 minutes. (It should not be brown.) Mix all ingredients for the filling and pour over the baked crust. Bake at 350 degrees for 25 minutes. After baking, dust the top lightly with powered sugar and cut into bars or squares. Makes 20 to 25 bars.

Orange Balls

1 **box vanilla wafers, crushed**	¼ **cup melted butter**
1 **cup chopped pecans**	1 **(6 ounce) can frozen orange**
1½ **cups powdered sugar,**	**juice (undiluted)**
divided	

Mix wafers, pecans and 1 cup powdered sugar. Add butter and orange juice. Mix well. Form into small balls and roll in remaining powdered sugar.

You can serve them at room temperature after preparing or put them in the refrigerator overnight and serve cold. Make the balls small as they are very rich!

Oatmeal Carmeletas

1 **cup flour**	1 **cup chocolate chips**
1 **cup oats**	½ **cup pecans**
¾ **cup brown sugar**	¾ **cup caramel ice cream**
½ **teaspoon baking soda**	**topping**
¼ **teaspoon salt**	3 **tablespoons flour**
¾ **cup melted butter**	

Combine flour, oats, brown sugar, baking soda, salt and butter. Place half of the mixture in the bottom of a 9 inch square pan. Reserve the other half for later. Press the mixture flat to cover the pan. Bake 10 minutes at 350 degrees. Remove from oven. Sprinkle 1 cup of chocolate chips over the baked mixture. Then sprinkle ½ cup of pecans on top of chocolate chips. Cover this with ¾ cup caramel ice cream topping, which has been mixed with 3 tablespoons of flour. Sprinkle reserved mixture on top of caramel layer. Crumble it to cover (do not flatten).

Bake at 350 degrees for 20 minutes or until golden brown. Chill 2 hours then cut into bars or squares. Chill another hour and serve cold. Must stay in refrigerator.

Peanut Butter Bars

2 **eggs, beaten**	1 **teaspoon vanilla extract**
½ **cup crunchy peanut butter**	1½ **cups sugar**
¼ **cup butter, melted**	1 **cup self-rising flour**

Cream all ingredients together. Pour into greased baking pan and bake at 350 degrees for 30 minutes or until golden brown.

Shoe Bottom Cookies

2	sticks butter, softened	1	pinch salt	
1	cup sugar	1	cup crushed pecans	
1	egg, separated		Sugar	
2	cups flour			

Cream butter and sugar. Add egg yolk and cream well. Sift flour and add to mixture. Add pinch of salt and mix until a stiff dough forms. Spread on ungreased 11 x 16 inch cookie sheet. Beat egg white with fork until foamy. Spread on top of dough. On top sprinkle crushed pecans and pat down with hands. Sprinkle just a little sugar on top. Bake at 250 degrees for approximately 30 minutes or until light brown. Cut into small squares while hot.

Tiger Stripe Bars

1	pound white chocolate vanilla almond bark	6	ounces semisweet chocolate chips
1	(12 ounce) jar crunchy or creamy peanut butter		

Line a 15½ x 10½ inch baking pan with waxed paper. Place white chocolate in a 3 cup measuring cup or 1½ quart microwave-safe bowl. Microwave on 70% power for 3 minutes or until melted. Stir before adding more cooking time. Add peanut butter, stir, and microwave on 70% power for 1 minute and stir until mixture is smooth and creamy. Pour mixture into paper-lined pan. In a 2 cup measuring cup, melt chocolate chips on 80% power for about 2 minutes. Stir well and drizzle over peanut butter mixture. Swirl with a knife to create tiger-stripe pattern. Chill until set and cut into squares.

Vanilla almond bark can be substituted for the white chocolate.

Pine Bark

1	stick butter	1	(12 ounce) package
1	cup light brown sugar		butterscotch chips
1	stack saltines		

Heat over to 400 degrees. Line cookie sheet with foil and spray with cooking spray. Place saltines on sheet in rows. Melt butter and sugar and boil 3 to 4 minutes. Drizzle sugar syrup over saltines and spread out evenly. Bake 4 minutes. Remove and sprinkle with chips — spread evenly over top of crackers with spatula. Cool in refrigerator for 1 hour. Break into pieces and serve.

Divinity

3	cups sugar	1	teaspoon vanilla extract
½	cup white corn syrup	½	teaspoon salt
¾	cup water	1	cup chopped pecans
2	egg whites		

Combine sugar, syrup, and water in a small saucepan and bring to a boil. Cover and let boil 3 to 4 minutes to avoid crystals. Continue cooking until a smooth amount drizzled into cold water will form a firm ball (this can take approximately 10 minutes). While the syrup is cooking, beat egg whites, vanilla extract, and salt in medium bowl on high speed until of the mixture forms stiff peaks when the beaters are lifted. Pour the syrup into the egg white mixture carefully, then continue beating until the mixture almost holds its shape. Fold in pecans, then drop by teaspoonfuls onto sheets of wax paper. Makes 40 to 50 pieces.

Do not attempt to make this on a humid day — it will break your heart.

Crock Pot Candy

1   (8 ounce) jar dry roasted peanuts, unsalted
1   (8 ounce) jar roasted peanuts, salted
1   (6 ounce) bag milk chocolate chips
1   (2 ounce) bar German chocolate, broken up into pieces
1½ pounds white bark

Put ingredients into a cold crock pot in the order listed. Cover and cook on low 3 hours. Do not remove lid. Turn off and cool slightly. Stir the candy and then drop by teaspoons on wax paper.

Pecans may be substituted for peanuts.

Recipe Contributors

Special Recognition given to those who contributed recipes for whom without, there would be no cookbook.

Acree, Charis
Adams, Lisa
Alford, Lisa L.
Alford, Lisa M.
Allen, Molly
Allred, Martha
Anderson, Ashley
Assaf, Chris
Ayers, Susan
Barth, Elizabeth
Bartlett, Gina
Bedingfield, Michele
Beedy, Jennifer Booker
Benefield, Kristy
Berman, Cindy
Black, Susan
Boatwright, Lisa
Booton, Ginger
Bradfield, Claire
Bridwell, Missy
Burch, Tolly
Cannady, Julie
Childress, Mary Lynn
Collins, Carla
Crawford, Kitty
Curry, Georgette
Davidson, Caroline
Davis, Betty
DeLoach, Blanche
Devane, Kendra
Doughman, Kelly
Downs, Stephanie Welch

Drinkard, Betty
Durand, Ida
Durand, Nancy
Eiler, Evans
Erickson, Laura
Estes, Page
Fagundes, Deana
Ferguson, Susan
Fincher, Kathryn
Foody, Susan
Fowler, Betsy
Franklin, Heather
Galster, Denise
Garrard, Laura
Gill, Julie
Godbehere, Chelle
Gore, Selma
Grace, Patti
Grovenstein, Lucy
Gulley, Kathleen
Harlin, Beth
Harman, Liz
Harrell, Diane
Holmes, Catherine
Hubbard, Kellie
Huff, Laura
Hull, Maria
Hunnicutt, Gail
Hunnicutt, Robyne
Hutchinson, Polly
Jackson, Cindy
Jones, Alynda

Recipe Contributors

Jones, Heather

Knight, Anna

Knight, Beth

Kurz, Elizabeth

Kyle, Ginny

Lanier, Cindy

Latham, Sherrie

Linch, Carole

Lynn, Debbie

Martin, Angie

Matheny, Alisa

McEachern, Phyllis

McGowan, Diane

Middlebrooks, Helen

Miller, Jayne

Moncrief, Stacy

Morman, Jessica

Morman, Sara

Morrison, Anise

Murphy, Kelli

Murray, Eloise

Murray, Teresa

Ochsenknecht, Angela

Oliver, Jan

Ormsby, Stephani

Patton, Kim

Payne, Tiffany

Pelham, Sarah

Pelham, Steve

Penn, Megan

Pippin, Darby Durand

Pitts, Emily

Pleasants, Catherine

Reams, Melanie

Riddle, Lauren

Roman, Brenda

Rowe, Jodi

Sargent, Debra

Shank, Lenora

Shedd, Laura

Skipworth, Cindy

Smith, Laura

Smith, LeTisha

Sneathen, Kimberly

Spinks, Tracy

Spivey, Christy

Stein, Beth

Stephens, Darlene

Stogner, Jennifer

Strickland, Shelley

Swiers, Christian

Taylor, Bit

Teaver, Nicole

Teaver, Patti

Thom, Martha

Thrailkill, Lynn

Trainer, Andrea

Trotter, Ruth Ellen

Upchurch, Jane

Vice, Kerri

Vinson, Alison

Walters, Elizabeth

Ward, Jodi

Westmoreland, Fiona

Wheeler, Marlene

Williamson, Teresa

Willis, Renae

Wroldsen, Jennifer

Young, Marty

Zachry, Ginger

JSL Members

Thank you to JSL members and sustainers for their support given to the production of Grits and Grace through promoting, taste testing, cooking, and various committee work.

Acree, Charis
Adams, Kelly
Adams, Lisa
Alford, Lisa L.
Alford, Lisa M.
Alford, Tracey
Allen, Molly
Allen, Patti
Allred, Martha
Anderson, Ashley
Anderson, Rocky
Assaf, Chris
Ayres, Susan
Bailey, Kristin
Baldwin, Judy
Barth, Elizabeth
Bartlett, Gina
Batchelor, Allison
Beall, Elizabeth
Beall, Sarah
Beason, Ann
Bedingfield, Michelle
Beedy, Jennifer Booker
Benefield, Kristy
Berman, Cindy
Black, Susan
Boatwright, Lisa
Boggus, Judy
Bohn, Terri
Booton, Ginger
Bowen, Carol
Boyd, Annette

Bradfield, Claire
Bradfield, Paige
Brannon, Deborah
Brazell, Jodi
Bridwell, Missy
Brooks, Kristen
Brown, Amanda
Brown, Julie
Burch, Tolly
Burdette, Debbie
Burdette, Nancy
Bushar, Linda
Cain, Kelly Durand
Callaway, Debbie
Camp, Molly
Cannady, Dana
Cannady, Jennifer
Cannady, Julie
Carmichael, Molly
Carson, Laura
Chaney, Julie
Chastain, Shelley
Childress, Mary Lynn
Cleaveland, Anna
Collins, Carla
Cook, Dee
Cooper, Wendy
Craig, Jane Alice
Crane, Irene
Crawford, Kim
Crawford, Kitty
Crews, Pam

Curry, Georgette
Dagenhart, Melissa
Daniel, Beth
Daniel, Linda
Daniel, Sue
Davidson, Caroline
Davidson, Ellen
Davis, Ashley
Davis, Betty
Davis, Dana
DeLoach, Blanche
Devane, Kendra
Doerr, Beth
Doerr, Kay
Doerr, Natalie
Doughman, Kelly
Downs, Stephanie Welch
Drinkard, Betty
Durand, Ida Solomon
Durand, Nancy Newman
Duttera, Sue
Edge, Deborah
Eiler, Evans
Erickson, Laura
Estes, Page
Evans, Lisa
Evans, Martha
Fagundes, Beth
Fagundes, Deana
Ferguson, Susan
Fincher, Kathryn
Fischer, Harriet
Foody, Suzanne
Forbus, Tammy
Fowler, Betsy
Franklin, Heather
French, Laura Leigh
Fritchley, Liza
Fuller, Laura Garrard
Galster, Denise

Genova, Anna Maria
Giesler, Linda
Gill, Valerie
Givins, Natalie
Godbehere, Chelle
Goodson, Katherine
Gordy, Jennie
Gore, Selma
Grace, Patty
Graham, Heather
Grovenstein, Lucy
Gulley, Kathleen
Guy, Jill
Hale, Natalie
Hancock, Ruth
Haralson, Donna
Harlin, Beth
Harman, Tammy
Harrell, Diane
Harris, Ellen Hudson
Henderson, Patty
Hensler, Connie
Holder, Barbara
Holle, Anita
Holliday, Julianne Lynn
Holmes, Catherine
Hubbard, Kellie
Hudson, Ida Callaway
Huff, Laura
Hull, Maria
Hunnicutt, Gail
Hunnicutt, Karyn
Hunnicutt, Robyne
Hunt, Holly
Hurst, Angela
Hutchinson, Polly
Ivey, Becky
Jackson, Cindy
Jackson, Karen
Jenkins, Ginger

Johnson, Jane

Johnson, Vicki

Jones, Alynda

Jones, Heather

Jones, Judy

Jones, Liz Harman

Jones, Zelda

Joseph, Emily

Kelly, Dorothy

Kibby, Karen

Knight, Anna

Knight, Beth

Knowlton, Sandra

Kornek, Casey

Kostilnik, Catherine

Kuerzi, JJ

Kurz, Elizabeth

Kyle, Virginia

Langford, Harriett

Lanier, Cindy

Latham, Sherrie

Linch, Carole

Long, Cammie

Long, Nancy

Lovejoy, Andrea

Lukken, Cindy

Lukken, Miriam

Lumpkin, Sherma

Lynn, Debbie

Macomber, Sally

Major, Becky

Malis, Sherry

Mallory, Jan

Mallory, Sarah Beth

Malone, Pat

Malone, Stacey

Mansour, Connie

Mansour, Emily

Marshall, Wendy

Martin, Angie

Matheny, Alisa

Mattox, Polly

McCoy, Lisa

McDonald, Gail

McEachern, Phyllis

McGowan, Diane

McKenzie, Cacky

Middlebrooks, Helen

Mike, Kami

Mike, Katherine

Miller, Jayne

Moncrief, Stacey

Moon, Amanda

Moore, Melissa

Morman, Jessica

Morman, Sara

Morrison, Anise

Morrow, Joanne

Murphy, Kelli

Myers, Kim

Ochsenknecht, Angela

Oliver, Gayle

Oliver, Jan

Ormbsy, Stephani

Parham, Louise

Patton, Kim

Payne, Tiffany

Pelham, Sarah

Penn, Megan

Pippin, Darby Durand

Pitts, Emily

Pleasants, Catherine

Prather, Cassandra

Rainey, Esther

Reams, Melanie

Reed, Ashley

Rice, Helen

Rich, Wilma

Riddle, Fay

Robinson, Mary Anna

Robinson, Suzanne
Rogers, Carole
Rogers, Patricia
Rogers, Shirra
Roman, Brenda
Roth, Rebecca
Rowe, Jodi
Russell, Ida
Sabet, Ann
Sargent, Debra
Schilly, Donna
Schirra, Cathy
Selbie, Joanna
Shank, Lenora
Shedd, Laura
Sheppard, Nancy
Sherrer, Rose
Simmons, Debbie
Skipworth, Cindy
Smith, Jerry
Smith, Laura
Smith, LeTisha
Smith, Marian
Smith, Michelle
Smith, Nicole
Sneathen, Kim
Solomon, Judy
Spinks, Tracy
Spivey, Christy
Stein, Beth
Stephens, Darlene
Stevens, Nancy
Stewart, Carol
Stich, Ann
Stogner, Jennifer
Strickland, Shelley
Stubbs, Margaret
Sweat, Diane
Taylor, Bit

Taylor, Carlene
Teaver, Nicole
Teaver, Patti
Tharpe, Andrea
Tharpe, Patrice
Thom, Martha
Thornton, Corinne
Thrailkill, Lynn
Trainer, Andrea
Trizzino, Jennifer
Trotter, Ruth Ellen
Turner, Christy
Tyler, Wendy
Upchurch, Jane
Upchurch, Kim
Vazquez, Debbie
Vice, Kerri
Vinson, Alison
Walters, Elizabeth
Walters, Karen
Ward, Jodi
Weiss, Jill
Westmoreland, Fiona
Wheeler, Marlene
Wheless, Mechelle
White, Christy
Wieland, Jan
Wiggins, Cathy
Wilder, Laurie
Wilkerson, Clairnelle
Williamson, Teresa
Willis, Renae
Willis, Susan
Wilson, Mary Anna
Wroldsen, Jennifer
Yates, Laurie
Young, Marty
Zachry, Ginger

Index

Index

Index

Index

Index

Index

Index

214

Index